# Conveyancing Protocol

Other titles available from Law Society Publishing:

**Commonhold**
Gary Cowen, James Driscoll and Laurence Target

**Conveyancing Checklists (2nd edn)**
Frances Silverman and Russell Hewitson

**Conveyancing Forms and Procedures (4th edn)**
Annette Goss, Lorraine Richardson and Michael Taylor

**Conveyancing Handbook (17th edn)**
General Editor: Frances Silverman, Consultant Editors: Annette Goss, Russell Hewitson, Peter Reekie, Anne Rodell, Michael Taylor

**Environmental Law Handbook (7th edn)**
Valerie Fogleman, Trevor Hellawell and Andrew Wiseman

**Leasehold Enfranchisement and the Right to Manage**
Christopher Sykes

**Property Development**
Gavin Le Chat

**Stamp Duty Land Tax (9th edn)**
Reg Nock

**Understanding Property Insurance**
Gerald Sherriff

**Understanding VAT on Property (2nd edn)**
David Jordan

Titles from Law Society Publishing can be ordered from all good bookshops or direct (telephone 0870 850 1422, email **lawsociety@prolog.uk.com** or visit our online shop at **www.lawsociety.org.uk/bookshop**).

# CONVEYANCING PROTOCOL

The Law Society

The Law Society

All rights reserved. No part of this publication may be reproduced in any material form, whether by photocopying, scanning, downloading onto computer or otherwise without the written permission of the Law Society except in accordance with the provisions of the Copyright, Designs and Patents Act 1988. Applications should be addressed in the first instance, in writing, to Law Society Publishing. Any unauthorised or restricted act in relation to this publication may result in civil proceedings and/or criminal prosecution.

Whilst all reasonable care has been taken in the preparation of this publication, neither the publisher nor the authors can accept any responsibility for any loss occasioned to any person acting or refraining from action as a result of relying upon its contents.

© The Law Society 2011

Forms in Appendix B are © The Law Society and are reproduced with the assistance of Oyez Professional Services Limited.

ISBN-13: 978-1-907698-05-7

Published in 2011 by the Law Society
113 Chancery Lane, London WC2A 1PL

Reprinted 2011 and 2013

Typeset by Columns Design XML Ltd, Reading
Printed by Hobbs the Printers Ltd, Totton, Hants

The paper used for the text pages of this book is FSC® certified. FSC (the Forest Stewardship Council®) is an international network to promote responsible management of the world's forests.

# Contents

| | |
|---|---|
| *Preface* | *vii* |
| *Acknowledgements* | *viii* |

**The Law Society Conveyancing Protocol**   1

   General obligations   1
   Interpretation   2
   Protocol framework   3
   Stage A: Instructions   4
   Stage B: Pre-exchange – submitting a contract   11
   Stage C: Prior to exchange of contracts   21
   Stage D: Exchange of contracts   25
   Stage E: Completion   28
   Stage F: Post-completion   30

**APPENDICES**

**A**   **A Guide to the Law Society Conveyancing Protocol**   33

**B**   **Law Society forms**   52

   (I)   TA6 Property information form   52
   (II)   TA7 Leasehold information form   64
   (III)   TA8 New home information form   70
   (IV)   TA10 Fittings and contents form   76
   (V)   TA13 Completion information and undertakings (2nd Edition)   80

**C**   **Standard Conditions of Sale (fifth edition) (including explanatory notes)**   84

**D**   **The Law Society's formulae for exchanging contracts by telephone, fax or telex**   104

CONTENTS

| | | |
|---|---|---|
| **E** | **The Law Society Code for Completion by Post** | **108** |
| **F** | **Certificate of title** | **113** |
| **G** | **Solicitors Regulation Authority warning cards** | **116** |
| | (I)   Warning Card on Property Fraud | 116 |
| | (II)  Warning Card on Money Laundering | 118 |
| | (III) Warning Card on Undertakings | 120 |
| **H** | **Law Society practice notes** | **122** |
| | (I)  Land Registry early completion practice note | 122 |
| | (II) Property and registration fraud practice note | 133 |
| **I** | **Law Society practice information** | **145** |
| | Accepting undertakings on completion following the Court of Appeal decision in *Patel* v. *Daybells* | 145 |

# Preface

The Law Society Conveyancing Protocol (the Protocol) has been developed to support all solicitors undertaking residential conveyancing and particularly those firms who have joined the Law Society Conveyancing Quality Scheme (the CQS). It has been drafted following consultation with user groups and its development has involved much debate and will no doubt generate more.

The timing of the introduction of the Protocol coincides with major changes that are likely to have significant impact on the conveyancing market. These changes include the move to outcomes-focused regulation, the advent of alternative business structures and changes to the professional indemnity insurance regime. These changes and proposed changes take place against the backdrop of a markedly changed residential property market and the challenges presented by the wider economy.

The intention of the Protocol is to set out the obligations of solicitors to their clients in such a way that it assists the client, in what is probably the biggest financial obligation they will make, to understand more about what they can expect in terms of process and service standards. It endeavours to ensure that the client is at the centre of the process and is kept fully informed throughout.

Lenders are obviously very important clients and it is equally important that lender clients are kept fully informed, particularly in relation to matters that may cause them to revise their lending decisions.

This Protocol takes a different format from those that preceded it. The focus is not only on the solicitor-to-solicitor contact but also encompasses the relationship with others in the process, such as estate agents, surveyors and mortgage brokers. In particular, the Protocol aims to make the standards expected of solicitors dealing with: lenders, buyers and sellers transparent to all.

We urge all firms undertaking residential conveyancing to join the CQS and practice in accordance with this Protocol. We would also like to invite solicitors to contribute feedback on the experience of using the Protocol so that it may be improved and refined in future editions.

Richard Barnett, Michael Garson, Paul Marsh and Jonathan Smithers
CQS Project Board
March 2011

# Acknowledgements

The Law Society would like to thank the following members of the Conveyancing and Land Law Committee and E-Conveyancing Task Force for their work in drafting the new Protocol and on revising the Code for Completion by Post and the Completion Information and Undertakings form:

- Richard Barnett
- Philip Freedman CBE QC
- Michael Garson
- Warren Gordon
- Jonathan Smithers.

The Law Society would also like to thank the following member of the Standard Conditions of Sale Joint Working Party for their contribution to updating the Standard Conditions of Sale:

- Richard Barnett
- Philip Freedman CBE QC
- Warren Gordon
- Elizabeth Ovey
- Graham Rounce
- Jonathan Smithers
- Malcolm Waters QC
- Graham White.

Tribute is paid to the late Trevor Aldridge QC for his work over many years in relation to the Standard Conditions of Sale.

At the Law Society thanks go to Sophie Brookes, Diane Latter and Natalie Taylor.

# The Law Society Conveyancing Protocol

This protocol is known as the Law Society Conveyancing Protocol (the Protocol).

The steps in the Protocol are not exhaustive and should not be regarded as a conveyancing 'checklist'.

## PROTOCOL: GENERAL OBLIGATIONS

The obligation to act in the best interests of the client takes precedence over this Protocol.

1. Disclose to the buyer/seller that there are professional obligations which apply to the sale and/or purchase. Obtain agreement and instructions to enable you to act in accordance with the terms and spirit of this Protocol.
2. Where acting for a lender as well as for a buyer/seller, the duties owed to the lender are no less important than they are for any buyer/seller, subject to the nature of the instructions.
3. There is potential for a conflict of interest to arise when acting for more than one party: sellers, buyers and lenders. Careful consideration must be given to this.
4. Endeavour to maintain vigilance to protect and guard against fraudulent or other illegal behaviour encountered in the conveyancing process.
5. Maintain high standards of courtesy and deal with others in a fair and honest manner.
6. Co-operate with others and treat them with respect.
7. Share information with others to assist in the efficient management of each transaction or chain of transactions. Requirements to provide and share information in each stage of the Protocol are subject to client confidentiality obligations. If the buyer/seller consents to the disclosure of information about the transaction, other transactions in the chain or any change in circumstances, this information should be disclosed. The buyer/seller should not be encouraged to withhold authority to disclose information unless there are exceptional circumstances.
8. Respond to all communications promptly or in accordance with agreed timeframes. Where something is to be addressed in a different order or by different means, this should be notified to those who are affected as soon as

reasonably possible. Steps required by the Protocol should be carried out as soon as reasonably possible.
9. Deal with transaction materials including correspondence, electronic or otherwise, efficiently and with care and consideration. Where parties agree to deal online, agree arrangements, for example, to acknowledge receipt. Where documents are submitted by post, submit draft documents in duplicate.
10. Ensure all incoming data is loaded on to the system and made available to the person dealing within a day of receipt, where any automated data handling or scanning of documents is used.
11. Use the most up-to-date versions of forms, formulae and codes provided by the Law Society. Follow the advice contained in SRA warning cards, guidance, Law Society practice notes and other practice information. Update forms to accord with changes in the law if these have not been updated by the Law Society.
12. Ensure proper arrangements are made for file management (including cover for absent colleagues) during any period of planned or unplanned absence.

**INTERPRETATION**

This section is designed to help with interpretation of the general obligations.

**1. Timetable**

The timing of each transaction will vary. The needs and requirements of the buyer/seller take precedence. A flexible approach by all will assist in achieving exchange of contracts and completion. In some transactions it may be appropriate to set some time parameters but these should only be agreed when all parties understand the factors that may affect the timescale and can make informed decisions regarding time requirements. For example, if a fixed period is suggested between instruction and exchange of contracts, both the buyer and the seller need immediately to be made aware of the length of time it may take for a mortgage offer to be issued, and the necessity for the buyer to have sufficient time to obtain the information and advice reasonably required to exchange contracts.

Other participants in the process, for example, estate agents, brokers and lenders, have important roles to play. Estate agents may have an understanding of associated transactions and may be able to assist in settling a realistic timetable. A framework for communication with others who may be able to contribute to the process should be considered and addressed in each case at the outset.

**2. The order of transactions**

For the purpose of this Protocol a straightforward residential sale and purchase transaction (freehold and leasehold) has been used as the model. The Protocol is only designed for use in residential transactions. It is recognised that the sequence for individual transactions will vary depending on the circumstances. The general obligations should nevertheless guide practitioners in these situations.

## 3. Transparency

Those participating in a transaction should recognise the value for all concerned in making the process transparent. This will assist clients and others to understand the process and this in turn should make the process more efficient.

## 4. Additional premiums and deposits

Local practice may vary as to the payment of premiums for indemnity insurances and the handling of deposit monies. This Protocol has deliberately not specified which party should pay the premiums nor how the deposit monies should be held. It cannot pre-judge the relative bargaining power of the seller and the buyer in any individual transaction.

## 5. Preferred practice

Use of this Protocol is considered preferred practice. It is only fully effective if both the seller's solicitor and the buyer's solicitor adopt it. However, if one party does not agree to adopt it, that does not prevent the use of the procedures by the other party.

## PROTOCOL FRAMEWORK

The Protocol sets out a framework of some of the work undertaken by the solicitors for the parties. To reduce concerns about delay whilst the solicitors on each side carry out the work they need to do, consideration should be given to creating a timing structure for the transaction. For example, allowing 10 working days after submission of a contract bundle for each party to report their current position in relation to the timetable for exchange and completion date and to disclose any potential problem or likely delay.

| Stage | Steps |
|---|---|
| A: Instructions | 1–18 |
| B: Pre-exchange – submitting a contract | 19–39 |
| C: Prior to exchange of contracts | 40–9 |
| D: Exchange of contracts | 50–9 |
| E: Completion | 60–6 |
| F: Post-completion | 67–70 |

CONVEYANCING PROTOCOL

STAGE A

# Instructions

| | Contact | Acting for the seller | Acting for the buyer | Contact |
|---|---|---|---|---|
| 1 | *Seller* | Once the property is available for sale, encourage the seller to formalise instructions as soon as possible in order to reduce delay when an offer has been accepted. | Encourage the buyer to formalise instructions as soon as possible in order to reduce delay when an offer has been accepted. | *Buyer* |
| 2 | *Seller* | Comply with all regulatory requirements, which include submitting an estimate of fees and disbursements and issuing a client care/retainer letter and any terms and conditions.<br><br>Settle costs on this basis.<br><br>Carry out and record:<br>• verification of identity and compliance with Money Laundering Regulations;<br>• conflict check;<br>• capacity of client check; and<br>• a scope of authority to act check, where there is more than one seller.<br><br>Request payment on account in relation to disbursements. | Comply with all regulatory requirements, which include submitting an estimate of fees and disbursements and issuing a client care/retainer letter and any terms and conditions.<br><br>Settle costs on this basis.<br><br>Carry out and record:<br>• verification of identity and compliance with Money Laundering Regulations;<br>• conflict check;<br>• capacity of client check; and<br>• a scope of authority to act check, where there is more than one buyer.<br><br>Request payment on account in relation to disbursements. | *Buyer* |

STAGE A: INSTRUCTIONS

| | Contact | Acting for the seller | Acting for the buyer | Contact |
|---|---|---|---|---|
| 3 | Seller | Enquire whether there are any adult occupiers other than the seller who may need to give consent. | Enquire whether there are any intending adult occupiers other than the buyer who may need to sign forms of waiver. | Buyer |
| | | Ensure the seller has written confirmation of:<br>• the name and status of the person who will carry out the work;<br>• the name of the regulated individual supervising the work; and<br>• the complaints procedure. | Ensure the buyer has written confirmation of:<br>• the name and status of the person who will carry out the work;<br>• the name of the regulated individual supervising the work; and<br>• the complaints procedure. | |
| 4 | Seller<br>Agent | Check whether the seller has property to buy and whether an offer has been accepted and whether there is any linked transaction or chain of transactions. | Check whether the buyer has property to sell and whether an offer has been accepted and whether there is any linked transaction or chain of transactions. | Buyer<br>Agent |
| | | | Check whether the buyer is in rented accommodation and the termination date of the tenancy or arrangements needed to give notice to terminate. | |
| | | | Advise generally as to shared or joint ownership if there is more than one buyer. | |

5

CONVEYANCING PROTOCOL

| | Contact | Acting for the seller | Acting for the buyer | Contact |
|---|---|---|---|---|
| 5 | *Seller*<br>*Agent*<br>*Broker* | Check whether the seller requires a mortgage offer in connection with any related purchase and, if so, whether:<br>• an application has been made; and<br>• a mortgage offer has been made. | Check whether the buyer requires a mortgage offer and, if so, whether an application has been made.<br><br>Suggest the buyer consults an independent surveyor for advice on valuation and survey.<br><br>Check whether a mortgage offer has been made or an 'in principle' offer received. | *Buyer*<br>*Agent*<br>*Broker* |
| 6 | | | Check which firm the prospective lender will be instructing if the buyer's solicitor will not be instructed by the lender. | *Buyer*<br>*Lender* |
| 7 | *Seller*<br>*Lender* | Obtain relevant written authority from the seller to deal with the seller's existing lender.<br><br>Obtain the title deeds, if any.<br><br>Obtain redemption figures and advise as to costs of obtaining redemption statements and any later updates. | Check availability, amount and source of deposit funds and purchase monies including whether a property is to be sold or mortgaged to provide funds.<br><br>Check whether any financial contribution is to be made by a third party and, if so, whether they require external advice. Consider the advice to be given to the lender about such contributions. | *Buyer*<br>*Lender* |

STAGE A: INSTRUCTIONS

| Contact | Acting for the seller | Acting for the buyer | Contact |
|---|---|---|---|
| | Examine the mortgage or other loans and consider obtaining a statement of account to ascertain redemption penalties or negative equity. If it is apparent that there is a negative equity or for some other reason the seller will not be able to discharge the registered charges from the proceeds of sale, discuss what actions need to be taken. | Suggest the buyer obtains quotations for buildings insurance and advise that the terms of any policy taken out must be compliant with the lender's requirements (where applicable). | |
| 8 | Establish the extent of, and title to, the land to be sold.<br><br>Registered title: obtain official copies and title plans for all titles to be sold and, where appropriate, official copies of registered documents.<br><br>Unregistered title: make an index map search and ascertain the whereabouts of the title deeds. | | |
| 9 *Seller* | Send a Property Information Form and a Fittings and Contents Form to the seller (with a warning that these documents may require later re-verification).<br><br>Explain to the seller the nature of the questions in the forms and ask the seller for documentation such as planning permissions, building regulation consents, plans, completion certificates and any guarantees. | | |

7

| Contact | Acting for the seller | Acting for the buyer | Contact |
|---|---|---|---|
| 10 | | Consider and advise in relation to any apparent defect in title or missing items in title documents, e.g. missing lease or discrepancies in names or addresses. | |
| 11 | | Consider how to deal with any restrictions appearing on the register. | |
| 12 | Seller<br>Landlord<br>Managing agent | Leasehold:<br>(1) Obtain the lease or official copy of the lease.<br>(2) Send a Leasehold Information Form (in addition to the Property Information Form) to the seller and obtain any documents that will be required, including a receipt for ground rent, service charge accounts and insurance details.<br>(3) Obtain from the seller the contact details for the landlord and/or managing agent and establish if a standard form of landlord/managing company replies to enquiries can be obtained and, if so, the cost.<br>(4) Consider submission of a questionnaire to the landlord/managing agent. | |

STAGE A: INSTRUCTIONS

| | Contact | Acting for the seller | Acting for the buyer | Contact |
|---|---|---|---|---|
| | | (5) Consider if any third parties will need to consent to the sale (e.g. landlord or management company). If so, establish the costs of obtaining such consent. It should generally be accepted that the seller will discharge this liability. | | |
| 13 | Seller | Check replies to enquiries and endeavour to obtain missing documentation. | | |
| 14 | | Consider which, if any, documents may need to be signed by an attorney and check whether powers of attorney are available. | Consider which, if any, documents may need to be signed by an attorney and check whether powers of attorney are available. | |
| | | Prepare any power that may be necessary. | Prepare any power that may be necessary. | |
| 15 | Seller | Ascertain the identity of all people aged 17 or over living in the property and ask about any financial contribution they or anyone else may have made towards its purchase or subsequent improvement. Consider whether their consent to the sale is required and whether independent advice is required. | | |
| 16 | Seller | **Optional** | | |
| | | Advise the seller about obtaining searches. | | |
| | | Consider which searches would be appropriate to obtain. If so instructed, instigate the searches. | | |

9

CONVEYANCING PROTOCOL

| Contact | Acting for the seller | Acting for the buyer | Contact |
|---|---|---|---|
| 17 | Review the costs estimate and revise if necessary, updating information regarding fees or disbursements. | Review the costs estimate and revise if necessary, updating information regarding fees or disbursements. | |
| 18 | Consider and advise in relation to any dependent purchase or sale. | Consider and advise in relation to any dependent purchase or sale. | |

STAGE B: PRE-EXCHANGE – SUBMITTING A CONTRACT

# STAGE B
# Pre-exchange – submitting a contract

The initial steps in Section B should generally commence within five working days of confirmation of the sale being received from the Seller, the Buyer or the Estate Agent as appropriate.

Details of any delay and explanation where appropriate should be communicated to the solicitor acting for the other party.

Following acceptance of an offer:

| | Contact | Acting for the seller | Acting for the buyer | Contact |
|---|---|---|---|---|
| 19 | *Seller* | Confirm the seller's instructions including checking for any incentives or other direct payments. Advise and record.<br><br>Confirm and update, where necessary, replies to enquiries if completed more than two months earlier. | Confirm the buyer's instructions including checking for any incentives or direct payments so that information can be given to the lender and others. Advise and record.<br><br>If not already carried out, advise on liability for SDLT.<br><br>Discuss advisability of having a survey carried out. | *Buyer*<br>*Lender*<br>*Surveyor* |
| 20 | *Agent* | Request a sales memorandum and particulars from the estate agent. Check terms are consistent with instructions. | | |

11

# CONVEYANCING PROTOCOL

| Contact | Acting for the seller | Acting for the buyer | Contact |
|---|---|---|---|
| 21 | Check the identity of the buyer's solicitor unless they are personally known to you. Follow the latest SRA and Law Society guidance and advice. Record and keep copies of evidence. | Check the identity of the seller's solicitor unless they are personally known to you. Follow the latest SRA and Law Society guidance and advice. Record and keep copies of evidence. | |
| 22 | Contact the buyer's solicitor to confirm instructions, the name of the conveyancer and the supervising solicitor or regulated principal. Provide the name of the seller, price agreed and state whether there is any related purchase. Confirm use of the Protocol. | Contact the seller's solicitor to confirm instructions, the name of the conveyancer and the supervising solicitor or regulated principal. Provide the name of the buyer, price agreed and state whether there is any related sale. Confirm use of the Protocol. | |
| 23 | Request details of the buyer's funding arrangements if not previously supplied. | Consider recommending that the buyer discloses funding arrangements if they have not previously disclosed them. | |
| 24 | If there is likely to be any delay in submitting a contract bundle, inform the seller, the buyer's solicitor and the estate agents. Prepare and submit to the buyer's solicitor a contract bundle which includes: | | |

STAGE B: PRE-EXCHANGE – SUBMITTING A CONTRACT

| Contact | Acting for the seller | Acting for the buyer | Contact |
|---|---|---|---|
| | (1) The draft contract incorporating the latest edition of the Standard Conditions of Sale. Note: The addition of further clauses to the contract is discouraged. Further clauses should not be included unless they are necessary to accord with current law, or specific and informed instructions have been given by the seller that inclusion of such clauses is necessary and they are required for the purposes of the particular transaction.<br><br>(2) If the title is registered:<br>  (i) official copies of the register and title plan (including official copies of all filed documents);<br>  (ii) an official copy of any registered lease; and<br>  (iii) where appropriate, an explanation of the seller's title, for example, if the name of the registered proprietor is different from the name of the seller.<br><br>Note: At the time of submitting the contract bundle:<br>• entries in the register of title should be less than six months old; and<br>• if any information needs to be updated (e.g. change of name, death of proprietor) the register should be rectified. | | |

| Contact | Acting for the seller | Acting for the buyer | Contact |
|---|---|---|---|
| | (3) If the title is unregistered:<br>(i) a land charges search against the seller and any other appropriate names;<br>(ii) an official search of the index map;<br>(iii) an epitome of title. Examine documents and mark copies or abstracts of all deeds that will not be passed to the buyer's solicitor as examined against the originals;<br>(iv) an examined abstract. Prepare, and mark as examined against the originals, copies or abstracts of all deeds prior to the root containing covenants, easements, etc. that may affect the property;<br>(v) generally such documents on which the seller can reasonably be expected to rely in order to deduce title (e.g. a certified copy of a grant of probate, a power of attorney, etc.).<br><br>Note: check all plans on copied documents are accurately coloured.<br>(4) Replies to enquiries with supporting documentation.<br>(5) Replies to the Fittings and Contents Form. | | |

STAGE B: PRE-EXCHANGE – SUBMITTING A CONTRACT

| Contact | Acting for the seller | Acting for the buyer | Contact |
|---|---|---|---|
| | (6) Planning permission and/or building regulation consents and completion certificates where any alterations or additions to the property have been carried out by the seller. Confirm that building plans will be delivered on completion where these are held. | | |
| | (7) Required consents (e.g. under restrictive covenants). The seller should supply these where available and when received they should be supplied to the buyer's solicitors. | | |
| | (8) In addition, in relation to leasehold property:<br>(i) replies to the Leasehold Information Form;<br>(ii) replies to enquiries made of the landlord/managing agents (where available) with accompanying documentation including three years' management accounts, a ground rent receipt, a buildings insurance policy with an up-to-date schedule and information about any required Deed of Covenant or other consent to assignment, etc.;<br>(iii) official copies of the freehold and intermediate titles;<br>(iv) a copy of the seller's share certificate for any landlord/management company where appropriate. | | |

15

# CONVEYANCING PROTOCOL

| | Contact | Acting for the seller | Acting for the buyer | Contact |
|---|---|---|---|---|
| | | (9) Any searches and enquiries made on behalf of the seller. | | |
| | | (10) If provided by the seller, an Energy Performance Certificate. | | |
| | | Consider also preparing a draft transfer either to attach to the contract or to submit with the contract. | | |
| 25 | | Request confirmation of the buyer's timescales for this and any related transaction or contemporaneous sale. | Request confirmation of the seller's timescales for this and any related transaction or contemporaneous purchase. | |
| 26 | Agent Seller | Inform the estate agent and the seller when the contract bundle has been submitted to the buyer's solicitor. | | |
| 27 | | Supply information about any related purchase by the seller and any other transactions in the chain where known, and subsequently notify of any change in circumstances. | Supply information about any related sale by the buyer and any other transactions in the chain where known, and subsequently notify of any change in circumstances. | |
| 28 | Seller | Provide the seller with the information received from the buyer's solicitor about any related sale by the buyer and any other transactions in the chain. | Provide the buyer with the information received from the seller's solicitor about any related purchase by the seller and any other transactions in the chain. | Buyer |

STAGE B: PRE-EXCHANGE – SUBMITTING A CONTRACT

| Contact | Acting for the seller | Acting for the buyer | Contact |
|---|---|---|---|
| 29 | If any document is unavailable or awaited then the contract bundle may be submitted with an explanation as to the likely timescale for it to be supplied. | On receipt of the contract bundle, notify the buyer that the contract bundle has been received. | |
| | | Notify the seller's solicitor if expecting to be instructed by the lender or communicate the identity of any other solicitors instructed by the lender when known. | Lender |
| 30 | | If searches are not being provided by the seller, make such searches as required. It is considered good practice to request these as soon as reasonably possible in the transaction unless instructed otherwise. If they are to be delayed for any reason, such as the buyer's chain being incomplete, notify the seller's solicitor. | |
| 31 | | If any further planning documentation is required, ascertain whether copies can be downloaded from any local authority or planning authority website. If any planning permissions were issued more than 20 years ago, the buyer's solicitor should obtain copies directly from the appropriate planning authority. | |

# CONVEYANCING PROTOCOL

| | Contact | Acting for the seller | Acting for the buyer | Contact |
|---|---|---|---|---|
| 32 | Agent Seller | Inform the seller and the estate agent of any difficulties likely to delay the exchange of contracts.<br><br>Obtain the seller's responses to additional enquiries. Explain that if inappropriate enquiries have been raised, answers need not be given.<br><br>Inform the buyer's solicitor that answers will not be given to inappropriate enquiries. | Raise only those specific additional enquiries required to clarify issues arising out of the documents submitted or which are relevant to the particular nature or location of the property or which the buyer has expressly requested.<br><br>Resist raising any additional enquiries, including those about the state and condition of the building, that have answers which are capable of being ascertained by the buyer's own enquiries, survey or personal inspection. Such enquiries should not usually be raised.<br><br>Indiscriminate use of 'standard' additional enquiries may constitute a breach of this Protocol. If such enquiries are submitted, the seller's solicitor is under no obligation to deal with them. Nor does the seller's solicitor need to obtain the seller's answers to any enquiry seeking opinion rather than fact. | |
| 33 | | | Report to the buyer on the documentation received and the results of investigations made.<br><br>Note: Do not wait for **all** documentation to be received before reporting to the buyer as this may delay raising any further enquiries. | Buyer |
| 34 | Seller | Take instructions and agree apportionments of the purchase price in respect of fittings and contents. | Advise the buyer as to the impact of an apportionment of the purchase price for fittings and contents on any mortgage offer and SDLT. | Buyer |

STAGE B: PRE-EXCHANGE – SUBMITTING A CONTRACT

| | Contact | Acting for the seller | Acting for the buyer | Contact |
|---|---|---|---|---|
| 35 | | Consider the position in relation to representation and proposed undertakings generally.<br><br>If the buyer's lender is not represented by the buyer's solicitor, consider what arrangements may be required. For example, where mortgage funds are being transmitted directly or evidence of discharge or undertakings for discharge are likely to be required by the buyer's lender's solicitor and the buyer's solicitor. | Consider the mortgage instructions from the lender or the lender's solicitor.<br><br>Check the offer conditions with the buyer. | Buyer |
| 36 | | | Consider the instructions from lenders in the CML Lenders' Handbook or the BSA Mortgage Instructions as applicable and make necessary disclosures including the buyer's full name and address and valuation assumptions. If the property is one to which the CML Disclosure of Incentives Form applies, obtain this and report to the lender. | Lender |
| 37 | | | Advise and take instructions from the buyer as to shared or joint ownership arrangements. | Buyer |
| 38 | Seller | Deal with any amendments to the contract after taking instructions if necessary. | Deal with any amendments to the contract after taking instructions if necessary.<br><br>Approve and return to the seller's solicitor:<br>• the provisions of the draft contract (including the buyer's full name and address); and<br>• any transfer. | Buyer |

19

| Contact | Acting for the seller | Acting for the buyer | Contact |
|---|---|---|---|
| 39 | Agree the contract and any transfer. | Agree the contract and any transfer. | |

## STAGE C

# Prior to exchange of contracts

| | Contact | Acting for the seller | Acting for the buyer | Contact |
|---|---|---|---|---|
| 40 | *Seller* | Obtain the seller's signature to the contract and the transfer if agreed.<br><br>Advise regarding the insurance and deposit arrangements in the contract. | Report to the buyer with the contract for signature.<br><br>Advise regarding the insurance and deposit arrangements in the contract.<br><br>Arrange for the buyer to transfer the deposit (preferably electronically and in a cleared form) to ensure there is no delay due to the clearance of cheques or electronic payments that take longer than a day. | *Buyer* |
| 41 | | Confirm the completion date and ensure the seller is aware of the obligation to give vacant possession. | Confirm the completion date and ensure the buyer is aware of the funding obligations. | |
| 42 | | | Consider whether to arrange for the signature of mortgage and SDLT return at the same time as the signature of transfer. Prepare a draft online SDLT return. | |
| 43 | | Ensure, so far as is possible, that the fullest information is made available as to the status of other transactions in the chain. | Ensure, so far as is possible, that the fullest information is made available as to the status of other transactions in the chain. | |

CONVEYANCING PROTOCOL

| | Contact | Acting for the seller | Acting for the buyer | Contact |
|---|---|---|---|---|
| 44 | | Confirm to the buyer's solicitor the form of discharge that will be given by the lender(s) (through their own solicitors if separate solicitors are acting for the seller's lender) so far as known.<br><br>Inform the buyer's solicitor if there are circumstances as to why identification of any seller's lender will not be supplied for the application to the Land Registry.<br><br>Consider whether undertakings are appropriate. If so, consider the type of undertaking to be offered in relation to any mortgage discharge required at completion.<br><br>Respond to the buyer's solicitor's enquiries.<br><br>Consider the SRA warning card on undertakings. | Consider the form of undertaking to be accepted in relation to the mortgage discharge required.<br><br>Consider the SRA warning card on undertakings. | |
| 45 | Seller Agent | Confirm the anticipated date for completion and arrange with the buyer's solicitor to check the date with others in any chain to see if it is agreed.<br><br>Request the client or estate agent to negotiate the date if required. | Confirm the anticipated date for completion and arrange with the seller's solicitor to check the date with others in any chain to see if it is agreed.<br><br>Request the client or estate agent to negotiate the date if required. | Buyer Agent |

STAGE C: PRIOR TO EXCHANGE OF CONTRACTS

| Contact | Acting for the seller | Acting for the buyer | Contact |
|---|---|---|---|
| 46 | Advise the seller about any apportionments that may be requested in addition to completion monies. Obtain the relevant supporting service charge or other documentation and receipts.<br><br>Advise the seller about continuing to make mortgage payments that are due prior to the completion date. | Remind the buyer about the availability of balance completion monies. Advise as to the date cleared monies are required for completion.<br><br>Suggest that the buyer investigates the cost and availability of buildings insurance so it is ready to be put in place on exchange or as required by the contract. | *Buyer* |
| 47 | | **Acting for the lender**<br><br>This part of the Protocol applies where the solicitor is instructed solely on behalf of the lender and not jointly for both the lender and the borrower.<br><br>If acting solely for the lender, the lender's solicitor is expected to:<br>• follow such parts of the Protocol as apply to that retainer; and<br>• take all action as is necessary to enable both the buyer's and the seller's solicitors to comply with the timescales. | *Lender* |
| 48 | | Establish whether any conditions of the mortgage offer remain to be performed, e.g. the availability of the mortgage valuation, or whether any matters need to be reported to the lender. | *Lender* |

| Contact | Acting for the seller | Acting for the buyer | Contact |
|---|---|---|---|
| 49 | | Consider whether there are any circumstances that are covered by SRA warning cards or Law Society practice notes. | |

## STAGE D

# Exchange of contracts

### STAGE D: EXCHANGE OF CONTRACTS

| | Contact | Acting for the seller | Acting for the buyer | Contact |
|---|---|---|---|---|
| 50 | | Consider the terms on which the deposit is to be held and by whom and advise the seller of potential consequences of default if, for example, the deposit is held to order. | Consider the terms on which the deposit is to be held and by whom and advise the buyer of potential consequences of default if, for example, the deposit is held to order. | |
| 51 | *Seller* | Use the appropriate Law Society formula for exchange by telephone or conduct a personal exchange. | Use the appropriate Law Society formula for exchange by telephone or conduct a personal exchange. | *Buyer* |
| | | Ensure adherence with the undertakings implied by such an exchange. | Ensure adherence with the undertakings implied by such an exchange. | |
| | | | Advise the buyer to arrange insurance cover immediately if the buyer is liable from exchange. | |
| 52 | *Seller*<br>*Agent*<br>*Chain* | Notify all relevant parties that exchange has taken place immediately after exchange of contracts. | Notify all relevant parties that exchange has taken place immediately after exchange of contracts. | *Buyer*<br>*Agent*<br>*Chain* |

25

## CONVEYANCING PROTOCOL

| Contact | Acting for the seller | Acting for the buyer | Contact |
|---|---|---|---|
| 53 | Reply to the questions in the Completion Information and Undertakings form and send to the buyer's solicitor. If not indicated previously, confirm the form of discharge that will be given by the lender so far as it is known. | Check replies to the Completion Information and Undertakings form, and the undertakings given for discharge against the register. Consider the Land Registry 'early completion' procedure and the effect of any restrictions on the title. | |
| 54 | Consider and reply to any additional requisitions on title raised by the buyer. | Raise any additional requisitions on title immediately following the exchange if permitted by the contract. | |
| 55 | | Prepare the SDLT return if not dealt with prior to the exchange. Advise the buyer to check it and, if satisfied, sign it. Use this as evidence even if proposing to file the return electronically. Prepare the online SDLT return if filing electronically. | |
| 56 | Provide the buyer's solicitor with a copy of the transfer executed by the seller to be delivered on completion. | Consider whether the transfer requires execution by the buyer following receipt upon completion or whether a duplicate (counterpart) should be obtained by the buyer in advance of completion. | |
| 57 | Obtain redemption figures for all financial charges revealed in the official copies or land charges register (where unregistered). | Prepare and submit at the appropriate time an official search of the register with priority at Land Registry (or land charges search if the land is unregistered) and a search of the bankruptcy register. | |

26

STAGE D: EXCHANGE OF CONTRACTS

| | Contact | Acting for the seller | Acting for the buyer | Contact |
|---|---|---|---|---|
| 58 | | | Send the certificate of title and/or requisition for funds to the lender (or the lender's solicitor if separately represented) promptly. Where the advance is to be sent by CHAPS, request wherever possible that the lender's advance is sent one working day before completion. Notify the buyer, if applicable, that interest may be charged by the lender from the day of transmission. | |
| 59 | *Seller* | Obtain the seller's instructions to pay the estate agent's fees from the sale proceeds. | Ask the buyer for completion monies in good time for completion or in a cleared form for balance of purchase monies and any other payments including SDLT and Land Registry fees. | *Buyer* |

CONVEYANCING PROTOCOL

STAGE E
# Completion

| | Contact | Acting for the seller | Acting for the buyer | Contact |
|---|---|---|---|---|
| 60 | *Seller Agent* | On the day before completion or as early as reasonably possible on the day of completion, consider whether there is likely to be any delay. If so, notify the buyer's solicitor and thereafter agree how communication will be handled during the course of the day until completion has taken place. | On the day before completion or as early as reasonably possible on the day of completion, consider whether there is likely to be any delay. If so, notify the seller's solicitor and thereafter agree how communication will be handled during the course of the day until completion has taken place. | *Buyer Lender* |
| 61 | | If completion is to be by post, comply with the Law Society Code for Completion by Post without variation unless instructions are given by the seller and are specific to the needs of the individual transaction. General exclusions of liability for obligations within the code will be viewed as a breach of this Protocol. | If completion is to be by post, comply with the Law Society Code for Completion by Post without variation unless instructions are given by the buyer and are specific to the needs of the individual transaction. General exclusions of liability for obligations within the code will be viewed as a breach of this Protocol. | |
| 62 | | Inform the buyer's solicitor of receipt of completion monies.<br><br>Completion. | Inform the seller's solicitor of the commitment of funds to the banking system or instructions given to the bank in accordance with the code.<br><br>Completion. | |

28

STAGE E: COMPLETION

| | Contact | Acting for the seller | Acting for the buyer | Contact |
|---|---|---|---|---|
| 63 | *Seller* *Chain* | Report completion to the seller and proceed with any related purchase transaction. If applicable follow the Law Society Code for Completion by Post. | Report completion to the buyer. If applicable follow the Law Society Code for Completion by Post. | *Buyer* *Chain* |
| 64 | *Agent* *Seller* | Notify the estate agent and/or any other key holder that completion has taken place and authorise immediate release of the keys. Notify the buyer's solicitor that completion has taken place and the keys have been released. Date and complete the transfer. Dispatch the completion documents including the transfer to the buyer's solicitor with any agreed undertakings. Send sufficient monies to the lender in accordance with any undertakings. | Date and complete the mortgage document. Confirm completion of the purchase and the mortgage to the buyer. Lodge the appropriate SDLT form with HMRC, preferably electronically, and pay any SDLT. On receipt of the certificate of notification from HMRC, lodge it with the application for registration at the Land Registry within the priority period of the official search. | *Buyer* *Agent* *HMRC* *Land* *Registry* |
| 65 | *Agent* *Seller* | Pay the estate agent's or property seller's commission if so authorised. | | |
| 66 | *Seller* | Account to the seller for any balance of the sale proceeds. | | |

29

CONVEYANCING PROTOCOL

STAGE F

## Post-completion

| Contact | Acting for the seller | Acting for the buyer | Contact |
|---|---|---|---|
| 67 *Lender* | Provide the buyer with sealed Form DS1 (and ID forms where applicable) as soon as it is received and obtain related discharge of undertaking. If the lender has discharged any registered charge by electronic means, notify the buyer's solicitor when confirmation is received from the lender. If none is received, contact the lender to obtain such confirmation. | Apply to the Land Registry for the discharge to be registered on receipt of any necessary release or discharge in Form DS1.<br><br>Request that the seller's solicitor explain the reason for delay if discharge of the seller's mortgage is not received prior to the lodgement of the application for registration at the Land Registry.<br><br>Request that an extension of the period for lodgement of the discharge is granted in order to avoid rejection of the application if there is a restriction when requisitioned by the Land Registry.<br><br>Inform the lender as to reasons for any delay in registration at the Land Registry. | *Lender* |

STAGE F: POST-COMPLETION

| Contact | Acting for the seller | Acting for the buyer | Contact |
|---|---|---|---|
| 68 | | If, under the 'early completion' policy, the discharge is received after notification that registration of the transfer has been completed:<br>• Check the contents of the title information document carefully.<br>• Supply a copy of it to the buyer and request that they check it.<br>• Confirm the position to the lender if required to do so by the lender's instructions. | *Buyer*<br>*Lender* |
| 69 | | When registration (whether subject to 'early completion' or not) has been effected:<br>• Check the title information document carefully, including the address for service.<br>• Supply a copy of the title information document to the buyer and remind the buyer to keep the address for service up to date.<br>• Ask the buyer to check the contents of the title information document.<br>• Advise the lender of completion of registration.<br>• Deal with any other documents, e.g. mortgage loan agreements, planning permissions, indemnity policies, etc. in accordance with the lender's instructions. | *Lender* |

31

| Contact | Acting for the seller | Acting for the buyer | Contact |
|---|---|---|---|
| 70 | | Take instructions as to any documents not being held by the lender, and if the documents are to be sent to the buyer or anyone else to hold on the buyer's behalf, inform the buyer of the need to keep the documents safely so that they will be available on a sale of the property. | *Buyer* |

# APPENDIX A

# A Guide to the Law Society Conveyancing Protocol

## 1. INTRODUCTION

The Law Society Conveyancing Protocol (the Protocol) is the Law Society's preferred practice for residential conveyancing transactions. It is designed for transactions that involve the transfer of freehold and leasehold residential properties. Firms that are members of the Law Society's Conveyancing Quality Scheme (the CQS) will be expected to follow the procedures set out in the Protocol in so far as this is appropriate for the particular transaction.

The first version of the Law Society National Conveyancing Protocol was introduced in March 1990 and it was last updated in 2004. The introduction of Home Information Packs (HIPs) cut across the Protocol. The abolition of HIPs, in addition to the inception of the CQS, provides the rationale for introducing a new protocol. This, the latest version of the Protocol is set out in a tabular, rather than a linear, process list form and it is hoped that this will enable clients as well as other professionals involved in the process to understand the stages of the process and what the other party is expected to do at any stage as well as indicating those points at which contact with others is most likely.

## 2. THE PROTOCOL

### 2.1 Date

The Protocol takes effect on 1 April 2011. Some transactions will be part way through at this date and, whilst the steps in the Protocol that have not already been carried out could be used in these transactions, the use of the Protocol will only be mandatory for CQS members who are commencing a transaction after this date.

### 2.2 Purpose

This Protocol is designed to bring structure and clarity to communication in residential property transactions.

Some parts of the conveyancing process are not governed by law but are shaped by convention and codes of practice; these develop over time and adapt to meet market practice. The Protocol aims to set out arrangements for the conduct of business between buyers and sellers and their respective solicitors on the basis of a set of agreed principles.

Others involved in the process will be able to better understand the set of processes involved and thereby access information about the stage that a particular transaction has reached. The Protocol can assist in explaining the steps that need to be followed to achieve exchange of contracts and completion of the transaction.

The buying and selling of a home is a non-contentious matter where both parties are broadly looking to achieve the same outcome: that is, the transfer of the home from seller to

APPENDIX A

buyer. Some of the 'general principles' set out at the beginning of the Protocol aim to encompass this fact and to improve communications and reduce unnecessary delays.

Previous iterations of the Protocol have focused on clarifying procedure and practice as between solicitors. This new version incorporates changes in practice and procedure but also faces outwards and aims to provide some transparency. The goal is to enhance the experience for solicitors as well as for the lender and lay clients.

Most sellers and buyers take part in conveyancing transactions rarely and are therefore not always familiar with all of the parts of the home buying and selling process. The Protocol is designed to assist solicitors to organise their work where it affects others and to better manage the expectations of sellers and buyers.

The Protocol follows the stages of a typical residential sale and purchase transaction. It does not prescribe the advice that solicitors offer but marshals work into agreed stages. It is hoped that its use will facilitate the interactivity on which the process relies. Where the terms of any transaction make the order of the Protocol inappropriate it is for the users of the Protocol to explicitly agree how they wish to vary the order of the Protocol or agree what alternative steps they wish to adopt.

Typically solicitors instructed by property sellers and buyers will be in contact with estate agents, brokers, lenders and surveyors. It is likely to assist the progress of a transaction if all those involved, including buyers and sellers, know the methodology that solicitors will be adopting in their conduct of the transaction.

## 2.3 Users

### CQS members

The Protocol has been developed and revised as part of the CQS scheme and it is a requirement of the scheme that members follow its obligations.

Under the CQS those who can become members are solicitors, licensed conveyancers and duly certified notaries public who practise residential conveyancing provided that they are employed by a practice regulated by the SRA. This includes any SRA regulated partnership, company, sole practitioner, limited liability partnership (LLP) recognised under s.9 of the Administration of Justice Act 1985 and legal disciplinary partnership (LDP) recognised under s.9A of the Administration of Justice Act 1985.

### Those who are not members of the CQS

Whilst it is possible for those who are not CQS members to use the Protocol, it is likely that CQS members will want to carry out checks of non-member firms in order to attempt to establish identity. The status of non-member firms will obviously be especially important in circumstances where professional obligations are involved (for example in relation to the giving of undertakings under the Law Society Code for Completion by Post). In dealing with non-CQS members it will be possible to use the Protocol but it will not be possible for CQS members to insist that it is used.

The Legal Services Act 2007 makes it an offence to carry on a 'reserved legal activity' through a person who is not entitled so to do. A solicitor should not deal with an unqualified person unless he has clear evidence that no offence under the Legal Services Act 2007 will be committed.

## 2.4 Scope of the Protocol

The Protocol is designed for use in residential transactions. The Protocol sets out the steps in the most basic of residential transactions. It is for use in freehold and leasehold sales and purchases of residential property.

It is designed to be used in matters that are wholly or primarily residential in nature. In most cases it should be relatively straightforward to establish whether the transaction is residential and one to which the Protocol should apply. However there will be a variety of matters where determination is not so simple. In order to establish whether or not the Protocol applies consider:

- the use of the property;
- the nature of the transaction;
- the nature of the parties;
- the nature of the contract;
- the nature of any mortgage.

Some of these categories may have areas of overlap or may conflict – it will be necessary to decide if the Protocol should apply to any transaction at its commencement. This should be discussed with the solicitor acting for the other party at the beginning. Even where it is not appropriate to use the Protocol CQS member firms should still act within the spirit of the Protocol.

## 2.5 Status of the Protocol

The Protocol has the status of preferred practice.

The Protocol sets out practice standards which are preferred practice and are not regulatory. However the Protocol does refer to other obligations including legislative, regulatory and other requirements, such as those of mortgage lenders. It is not exhaustive in this regard.

The Protocol contemplates only a very simple transaction and there may be many matters in a transaction that may make some deviation from the Protocol desirable or necessary. It does not include the alternative and additional requirements involved in many kinds of transactions.

This Protocol has been issued by the Law Society for the use and benefit primarily of CQS members. The Protocol sets out the Law Society's view of preferred practice in residential conveyancing. It is not intended to be the only standard of good practice that solicitors can follow.

Where the Protocol refers, for example, to the Code for Completion by Post and the formulae for exchange of contracts it should be remembered that use of these carries the force of professional obligations.

There are specific conduct rules that regulate conveyancing transactions (Solicitors' Code of Conduct 2007, rules 3.07–3.15).

The nature of the transaction, instructions from clients, changes in regulation, statute law or case law may be matters that will take precedence over the Protocol.

It is the responsibility of users of the Protocol to decide when it is appropriate and when it is not appropriate to follow the Protocol. CQS member firms should still act within the spirit of the Protocol if an individual case/circumstance dictates that they need to move away from it.

If the Protocol is not followed in a relevant transaction consideration should be given to how this would be justified to the CQS or to the Solicitors Regulation Authority (SRA) or other regulatory body. If not using the Protocol is appropriate in the context of a particular retainer consider making a note of the explanation for its non-use on file.

APPENDIX A

If solicitors adopt the Protocol then they agree to substantially comply with its terms and with the spirit of the process outlined. Any material breach or repeated breaches reported in one or more transactions may result, in the first instance, in the Law Society requiring an explanation from the Senior Responsible Officer (SRO) appointed under the CQS procedures. Repeated cases of serious default will be monitored and where necessary adjudicated under the membership rules of the CQS and may result in expulsion from membership of the CQS.

The Protocol is designed to drive up standards and the quality of work carried out. So, for example where the contract bundle documents are not checked or are incomplete the seller's solicitor will have failed to meet the standards required if this is not stated and the missing documents are not supplied as soon as reasonably possible.

## 3. THE GENERAL PRINCIPLES OF THE PROTOCOL

### 3.1 Overview

The Protocol begins with a list of governing principles that are 'general obligations'.

1. Disclose to the buyer/seller that there are professional obligations which apply to the sale and/or purchase. Obtain agreement and instructions to enable you to act in accordance with the terms and spirit of this Protocol.

Clients need to be advised of the basis on which the work will take place. It is important for the client to understand that, whilst acting for them, there are overriding professional obligations. This provision gives a specific and positive obligation to seek instructions and set out the limits of the retainer particularly in relation to obtaining the client's agreement to act as the Protocol provides.

2. Where acting for a lender as well as for a buyer/seller, the duties owed to the lender are no less important than they are for any buyer/seller, subject to the nature of the instructions.

Lenders are important clients and solicitors need to take their instructions very seriously. This is particularly critical in relation to matters that might cause the lender to reconsider its proposals to lend on particular terms, for example in relation to the source of funds over and above the mortgage monies. When acting for lender and borrower the duties owed to both clients are equally important.

3. There is potential for a conflict of interest to arise when acting for more than one party: sellers, buyers and lenders. Careful consideration must be given to this.

Whilst solicitors will be aware of the current rules relating to conflicts the provisions under the new system of outcomes-focused regulation (OFR) proposed by the SRA may change what is permissible as from 6 October 2011.

4. Endeavour to maintain vigilance to protect and guard against fraudulent or other illegal behaviour encountered in the conveyancing process.

Solicitors are the gatekeepers of the process and must endeavour to establish the identities of those dealing – both clients and those acting on the other side. It is important to be vigilant to guard against fraudulent or any other illegal behaviour by any participant in the conveyancing process.

Paragraph 4 is no more than a restatement of obligations but it highlights the importance of these obligations.

## A GUIDE TO THE LAW SOCIETY CONVEYANCING PROTOCOL

5. Maintain high standards of courtesy and deal with others in a fair and honest manner.
6. Co-operate with others and treat them with respect.

The transaction is a non-contentious one. The obligation to act in the best interests of the client is paramount. Consider the main objective of the client in the transaction. The steps of the Protocol should always be followed with care and consideration to all participants.

7. Share information with others to assist in the efficient management of each transaction or chain of transactions. Requirements to provide and share information in each stage of the Protocol are subject to client confidentiality obligations. If the buyer/seller consents to the disclosure of information about the transaction, other transactions in the chain or any change in circumstances, this information should be disclosed. The buyer/seller should not be encouraged to withhold authority to disclose information unless there are exceptional circumstances.

One of the factors in achieving an uneventful and predictable conveyancing transaction is having good quality communication between all of those involved. This obligation requires that information is shared with others to assist in the efficient management of each transaction or chain of transactions. This only applies in so far as this is permitted by the client. Rule 4 of the Solicitors' Code of Conduct 2007 requires that care must always be taken to avoid any breach of the duty of confidentiality owed to the client. The client is entitled to refuse to permit you to disclose any information and this will outweigh obligations under the Protocol. However, clients should be encouraged only to withhold the authority to disclose in exceptional circumstances.

Transactions are often complicated by the related purchase or sale of another property that must be conducted simultaneously. This position could be replicated a number of times over in a chain of related transactions. Chains will impact on the use of the Protocol particularly in relation to timing but will make the principles relating to disclosure even more important. Understanding and taking account of the fact that everyone in the chain is reliant on each other is an important factor in improving the quality of the process. The issue of the provision of information across chains is likely to be the most contentious in the context of confidentiality requirements. The interdependence of transactions arises not only in relation to purchases and sales that depend on one another but in relation to other transactions such as the sale of investments to finance a deposit, the conclusion of a divorce or the issuing of a grant of probate.

The personal circumstances of parties may change unexpectedly or by reason of unemployment, holidays, illness or family events. Problems may arise in the course of a transaction concerning funding, survey, or defects in title. In all of these situations parties will want to be aware of the position as soon as it is known and be clear as to the cause of any delay or breakdown in progress and how long it may take to resolve. The process therefore aims to commit the seller and buyer and their legal advisers to an agreed method of dealing. Those adopting the Protocol will be encouraged to ensure that, where the duty of client confidentiality allows, the timely sharing of information and co-operating with their counterparts leads to enhancement of the client experience and in the reduction of time and wasted expenditure.

This is a difficult area – the duty of confidentiality may come into conflict with the requirement for disclosure but the duty of confidentiality is the paramount obligation. If the client asks that the seller's agent and solicitor are not told that the client no longer has a buyer for their related sale or has had their mortgage application rejected then this must take precedence over the obligation to keep everyone informed.

## APPENDIX A

Management of information is as important as the information itself. If the seller is told what the buyer is doing to resolve the problem, they may perhaps be more likely to wait for resolution, than they would if they discovered at a later date that the information had been withheld.

8. Respond to all communications promptly or in accordance with agreed timeframes. Where something is to be addressed in a different order or by different means, this should be notified to those who are affected as soon as reasonably possible. Steps required by the Protocol should be carried out as soon as reasonably possible.

With a view to avoiding or reducing any unnecessary delay, it is important to respond to all communications promptly. Where something is to be dealt with in a different order or by alternative means this is to be made clear to those who are affected as soon as it is possible to do so. The Protocol recommends that timeframes are agreed where possible.

9. Deal with transaction materials including correspondence, electronic or otherwise, efficiently and with care and consideration. Where parties agree to deal online, agree arrangements, for example, to acknowledge receipt. Where documents are submitted by post, submit draft documents in duplicate.

Increased use of electronic communications gives rise to the necessity to agree arrangements for submission of and response to documents. The obligation to submit in duplicate is to counter a growing trend for some firms to submit only one part of the contract and immediately ask their clients to sign the other part. This increases the risk of exchange not being effected in accordance with s.2 of the Law of Property (Miscellaneous Provisions) Act 1989 as the two parts are less likely to be identical.

10. Ensure all incoming data is loaded on to the system and made available to the person dealing within a day of receipt, where any automated data handling or scanning of documents is used.

This is an obligation to ensure that information is reliable and up to date. It primarily applies to those solicitors using case management systems or other automated data handling systems and scanning and distribution systems. It is not an obligation on all.

11. Use the most up-to-date versions of forms, formulae and codes provided by the Law Society. Follow the advice contained in SRA warning cards, guidance, Law Society practice notes and other practice information. Update forms to accord with changes in the law if these have not been updated by the Law Society.

How many firms simply stick to what they know but do not adjust their procedures to take account of changes in practice or in the law? This is a positive obligation to use the most up-to-date versions of forms and to take account of practice materials and to make appropriate changes to the forms in accordance with changes in the law.

The Law Society cannot always react instantly if there is a change in law or procedure perhaps following judicial decisions so again it is a positive obligation to make a change if it is properly required.

12. Ensure proper arrangements are made for file management (including cover for absent colleagues) during any period of planned or unplanned absence.

If the person dealing with the transaction is absent for any reason such absence should be covered by another. The Protocol requires that proper arrangements are put in place for file management.

## 3.2 Interpretation

There is a section in the Protocol about the interpretation of the general obligations. This also demonstrates what is not in the Protocol. The obligations are set out as follows:

### 1. Timetable

The timing of each transaction will vary. The needs and requirements of the buyer/seller take precedence. A flexible approach by all will assist in achieving exchange of contracts and completion. In some transactions it may be appropriate to set some time parameters but these should only be agreed when all parties understand the factors that may affect the timescale and can make informed decisions regarding time requirements. For example, if a fixed period is suggested between instruction and exchange of contracts, both the buyer and the seller need immediately to be made aware of the length of time it may take for a mortgage offer to be issued, and the necessity for the buyer to have sufficient time to obtain the information and advice reasonably required to exchange contracts.

Other participants in the process, for example, estate agents, brokers and lenders, have important roles to play. Estate agents may have an understanding of associated transactions and may be able to assist in settling a realistic timetable. A framework for communication with others who may be able to contribute to the process should be considered and addressed in each case at the outset.

This section seeks to encourage the setting of realistic and achievable timetables so that clients know what to expect in terms of timing. The timetable for the transaction is probably one of the most important aspects of the Protocol to the client.

The Protocol sets out a framework for some of the tasks undertaken by the solicitors for the parties. To reduce concerns about delay whilst the solicitors on each side carry out the work they need to do, consideration should be given to creating a timetable structure for the transaction. For example, allow 10 working days after submission of a contract bundle for each party to report their current position in relation to the timetable for exchange and completion date and to disclose any potential problem or likely delay.

The timing cannot be precise for each stage but generalised indications are modelled in the Protocol. Where expectations cannot be met it is the responsibility of the solicitor to inform his client and relevant connected parties of the position so that people are kept informed.

### 2. The order of transactions

For the purpose of this Protocol a straightforward residential sale and purchase transaction (freehold and leasehold) has been used as the model. The Protocol is only designed for use in residential transactions. It is recognised that the sequence for individual transactions will vary depending on the circumstances. The general obligations should nevertheless guide practitioners in these situations.

### 3. Transparency

Those participating in a transaction should recognise the value for all concerned in making the process transparent. This will assist clients and others to understand the process and this in turn should make the process more efficient.

### 4. Additional premiums and deposits

Local practice may vary as to the payment of premiums for indemnity insurances and the handling of deposit monies. This Protocol has deliberately not specified which party should pay the premiums nor how the deposit monies should be held. It

# APPENDIX A

cannot pre-judge the relative bargaining power of the seller and the buyer in any individual transaction.

In the initial consultation with local law societies, a number suggested that the Protocol should contain an obligation that sellers (or buyers) should always pay premiums particularly for chancel repair policies or indemnity insurance premiums.

The drafting committee decided that it was not proper to make specific rules or guidance on this. Different solicitors take different views as to whether policies are necessary or useful. An obligation that one (or other) party always pays would shift the balance against that party.

The economic bargain between seller and buyer on price may impact on their willingness to contribute. The Protocol may bind solicitors but it cannot bind the clients who would be paying the premium.

The consultation process revealed that practice regarding the payment and acceptability of deposits of varying amounts differed.

The Protocol does not preclude the adoption of standard provisions in relation to these matters to meet local convention.

## 3.3 Notes

(i) The obligation to act in the best interests of the client takes precedence over the Protocol.
(ii) The steps in the Protocol are not exhaustive and should not be regarded as a conveyancing 'checklist'.
(iii) In some cases the Protocol offers options for a party to adopt according to their preference and in others there is a default position to be followed.
(iv) The Protocol does not set out legal advice and is no substitute for necessary legal advice nor does it set out all the work that needs to be undertaken in order to carry out competently what is required to meet professional and legal obligations.
(v) The Protocol is a framework for the parties that can be adapted by prior agreement to suit the needs of the parties in any particular situation.
(vi) The Protocol does not constitute legal advice, nor does it necessarily provide a defence to complaints of misconduct or of inadequate professional service. While care has been taken in the drafting of the Protocol the Law Society will not accept any legal liability in relation to it.

## 3.4 Terms used in the Protocol

(i) The term 'solicitor' in the context of the Protocol includes solicitors and licensed conveyancers.
(ii) Terms such as 'seller' and 'buyer' include one person or more than one person.
(iii) 'He' includes 'she'.
(iv) Where reference is made to the CML Lenders' Handbook this only applies where the lender is a full member of the CML and instructs using the CML Lenders' Handbook. Where a lender has elected to instruct under the provisions of the BSA Mortgage Instructions the Protocol should be read as though referring to the corresponding provisions in the BSA Mortgage Instructions. Where a lender instructs using its own instructions, again the Protocol should be read as though referring to the corresponding provisions in the CML Lenders' Handbook if appropriate.

## 4. OPERATIONAL INFORMATION

### 4.1 Stage A: Instructions

At this early stage in the process the main steps relate to preparation for later stages.
It is a regulatory requirement that:

- in appropriate cases the legal capacity of the client is checked in relation to the transaction;
- there is no conflict of interest that may preclude the solicitor or the firm from acting in the transaction.

Since the earlier versions of the Protocol there are now more obligations in relation to checking the identities of the parties and others in the process and completeness of funding arrangements.

The obligations in relation to checking or attempting to check a client's identity are a regulatory matter rather than a Protocol requirement. Lenders have their own requirements in relation to identity checks to be carried out against borrowers. It is important to keep appropriate records of the checks made in relation to a prospective client's identity. The regulations in this regard are designed to be a precaution against mortgage fraud and money laundering.

For these reasons it is also necessary to check the identity of the solicitor acting for the other side.

Recent changes have been made to the CML Lenders' Handbook for England and Wales to provide that lenders are entitled to ask for the details of the other side's solicitors at the beginning of the transaction.

Note also the requirements of the CML Lenders' Handbook for England and Wales Part 1, which provides:

> A3.2 If you are not familiar with the seller's solicitors or licensed conveyancers, you must verify that they appear in a legal directory or they are currently on record with the Law Society or Council for Licensed Conveyancers as practising at the address shown on their note paper.

In addition to identity it is also important to consider the position of the parties as between themselves particularly when acting for buyers.

*Buyers*

If a property is being bought by more than one person the buyers' solicitor will need to take detailed instructions. Buyers should be advised as to the ways in which property can be held in joint names and whether an express declaration of trust should be drawn up. The buyers' solicitor should consider how the beneficial interests will be recorded in the transfer. Whether this is to be recorded by a trust deed or through the transfer itself, the buyers will need to sign the document as a deed. A copy of this should be retained at a later date before application to the Land Registry for registration. Buyers should be made aware that clarifying these matters at this stage may avoid misunderstandings, cost and expense at a future date or in the event of disagreement as to the nature of the trust.

If there are adults who intend to occupy the property but who will not be owners their consent will be necessary in order to ensure that the lender's rights are binding on them. In this respect it may be appropriate for them to be offered the opportunity to take independent advice.

When acting for a buyer establish whether there will be a sale or mortgage of any other property that will be related to the purchase. If the buyer is in rented accommodation establish

APPENDIX A

the possible termination dates of the tenancy, the period of notice and what arrangements need to be made to give notice.

*Sellers and buyers*

If there is more than one client, for example where the property is in joint names, it is important to check the scope of the authority to act in this situation. You need to have instructions from both clients even if authority is given for one to act on behalf of them jointly for day-to-day communications.

At an early stage the seller's solicitor should obtain the written authority from the client to deal with the lender authorising the release of the deeds and providing a redemption statement.

*Apparent title defects*

The obligation on the seller's solicitor, at an early stage in the process, to 'consider and advise in relation to any apparent defect in title or missing items in title documents, e.g. missing lease or discrepancies in names or addresses' aims to assist in accelerating the removal of defects that can cause delays. Management company restrictions, missing evidence of rights of way, mismatching of names of registered proprietors and sellers, need to be investigated or rectified by the seller's solicitor. If the registered title shows entries that will necessitate the transfer being signed by at least two trustees or a trust corporation this needs to be considered at an early stage. Other matters that can lead to delay include a requirement for the landlord's consent in a leasehold transaction or the use of powers of attorney. If an attorney is involved produce a certified copy of the power at an early stage; remember an attorney must act with at least one other person to overreach beneficial interests in land and that the Land Registry has detailed identity requirements in relation to attorneys.

Where a client is selling a house, even before a buyer is located, it assists if the seller's solicitor ensures that terms and conditions, identity documents and such like are dealt with. Downloading official copies may reveal that the register needs to be updated – if, for example, a grant of probate needs noting or if there has been a change of name by deed poll or marriage.

Notwithstanding the above the primary obligation for establishing title remains with the buyer's solicitor and it will remain the obligation of the buyer's solicitor to report on title to his lay client and any lender client.

If the property is leasehold, the seller should supply the information they can about service charges, insurance and ground rent, make enquiries about the landlord and/or managing agents. Sellers will not necessarily wish to put together the full package before the chain is complete, as a result of the cost of doing so and the need to update if finding a buyer takes a long time, but it will assist the process if sufficient information is obtained so that at the minimum it is known where to go and how much it will cost when the need for this information arises.

The seller's solicitor may also advise the seller about the desirability of obtaining searches in advance.

### 4.2 Stage B: Pre-exchange – submitting a contract

This stage primarily involves the collation of the material necessary to provide a bundle of documents for the buyer's solicitor. The obligations are not wholly prescribed and offer an element of choice. In relation to official copies, these could be obtained by the buyer and it is possible to agree that this will take place. However in circumstances where the seller may give instructions at an early stage, before there is a buyer, requiring the seller's solicitor to obtain the official copies, registered title plan and copies of other registered documents enables them to comply with the requirements to start to address title issues at an early stage.

There is no obligation on sellers to obtain search results for buyers but they may if they wish. If they do so there is no obligation on a buyer's solicitor to accept such searches.

Sellers are obliged to provide building regulation documents and planning consents where they themselves have had the work carried out to the property. Where the seller holds no further information and the buyer's solicitor requires additional copy consents they should establish whether these are available from the local planning authority and pursue the matter direct where such consents are older than 20 years.

### 4.3 Stage C: Prior to exchange of contracts

The seller's solicitor should provide as much documentation as is possible at the outset and should, without further prompting from the buyer, apply for and supply filed documents. Official copies should be less than six months old at the time of submission. This obligation is designed to lessen the possibility of alterations to the register having taken place between production of official copies, submission of papers and pre-completion priority searches.

The seller's solicitor has an obligation to rectify the register to deal with any updating including a change of name on the death of a proprietor.

The joint Law Society and Land Registry Practice Note: Property and Registration Fraud (11 October 2010) points out that transactions following the death of a registered proprietor are at greater risk from fraudsters posing as executors or the deceased where no note has been made on the register. Updating the register currently carries no application fee.

When the buyer's solicitor receives the contract bundle, the buyer's solicitor is required to notify the seller's solicitor if he is instructed by the buyer's lender or if not to give details of the firm so instructed.

The Protocol requires the seller's solicitor to inform the buyer's solicitor if they are not able to comply with the Land Registry's requirements for any lender for the purposes of the buyer's application for registration to the Land Registry (Land Registry Practice Guide 67: Evidence of identity – conveyancers). It is important that these issues are addressed prior to exchange. Even where it is expected that the discharge will be made electronically, if this is not possible it is likely that the discharge will be made by paper DS1 triggering the identification requirements and this will not usually be known until after exchange and sometimes after completion. See the new provisions in the Law Society Code for Completion by Post.

*Planning permission/building regulations*

Planning permissions and building regulation consents should be produced where work has been undertaken during the period of ownership of the seller.

Where the buyer's solicitor requires copies of other planning permissions or building regulation consents, he should first check the local authority or planning authority website to seek to download documents directly (for which there is usually no charge) before requesting these from the seller's solicitor.

If planning permissions or building regulation consents are more than 20 years old, the buyer's solicitor should expect to apply directly for (and pay for where necessary) any copies required.

*Searches*

Following submission of papers, the buyer's solicitor would be expected to request searches, as soon as reasonably possible. If they are to be delayed (for example if the chain of transactions is incomplete) then the seller's solicitor should be notified. It is worth noting that

APPENDIX A

some solicitors routinely do not institute searches until the mortgage offer is made available. This may save the buyer money but can lead to delay so it is important that the seller's solicitor is made aware of this practice as soon as possible.

It is preferred practice for the buyer's solicitor to ensure that the buyer is aware of the limitations of replies to search enquiries.

*Enquiries*

The buyer's solicitor should raise only those specific additional enquiries that are required to clarify issues arising out of the documents submitted or which are relevant to the particular nature or location of the property or which the buyer has expressly requested.

They should resist raising any additional enquiry including those about the state and condition of the building which is capable of being ascertained by the buyer's own enquiries or survey or personal inspection. The Protocol includes the longstanding advice of the Law Society as to the type of enquiries to be raised.

It is preferred practice for the buyer's solicitor to ensure that the buyer is aware of the limitations of replies to enquiries and the warranties that should properly be sought.

*Purchase price, deposit and incentives*

The buyer's and seller's solicitors should advise as to the likely impact on the mortgage offer and the stamp duty land tax liability where apportionment of the purchase price for fittings and contents is suggested. On the information given is the suggested apportionment plainly unreasonable? Might it affect the percentage being borrowed as lenders will generally only take into account the price paid for the property and not any contents? See **www.hmrc.gov.uk/manuals/sdltmanual/sdltm04010.htm**.

At the present time when there are real constraints on borrowers, with particular problems for first time buyers obtaining mortgages, many parents, grandparents and others are providing contributions towards the purchase price of the property. Where it becomes apparent that not all of the deposit or purchase monies, other than the mortgage monies, are coming directly from the buyer there are several issues to be considered:

- Does the lender know?
- Is this a matter that should be reported to the lender?
- How is such a contribution to be recorded?
- Should those proposing to advance such monies be advised to first take their own independent advice?

If the property is a new build or new conversion the buyer's solicitor needs to check with the client to see whether any incentives have been provided by the developer and obtain a completed CML Disclosure of Incentives Form completed by or on behalf of the developer from the seller's solicitor. Similar payments may apply in relation to other sales and the client should be asked whether they have received or made any direct payment or intend to do so with the other party.

Such matters must be disclosed to the lender.

If the deposit is held by the buyer's solicitor 'to the order' of the seller's solicitor the Protocol requires the parties' solicitors to consider the terms on which it is held.

Usually if no other discussions or communications have taken place, the terms on which the deposit is held might effectively be that an undertaking has been given by the buyer's solicitor that he is holding the deposit in his client account and will send it to the seller's solicitor as soon as this is requested, notwithstanding any argument between the buyer and seller as to legal entitlement to it.

## 4.4 Stage D: Exchange of contracts

*Points to consider*

When the parties are almost ready to exchange it is necessary to check the suggested completion dates with the clients, other solicitors in the chain and, where appropriate, any estate agents.

If there is more than one transaction for a client in a chain consider the order of exchanging – advise the client of the risks of exchanging on a purchase in advance of exchanging on a sale. The aim is to exchange on both transactions simultaneously but this is not always possible.

There is the option for the buyer's and seller's solicitors to deal with the transfer prior to exchange. Many solicitors acting for the seller may draft the transfer and obtain the seller's signature to it along with the sale contract in order to reduce the time required between exchange of contracts and completion. If this is done, the seller's solicitor should submit a copy of the executed transfer to the buyer's solicitor in advance in order to ensure that any corrections that may be required are undertaken prior to completion.

Although the obligation is repeated in the Law Society Code for Completion by Post, the seller's solicitor should provide replies to the questions in the Completion Information and Undertakings standard Law Society form at exchange. At present, it is common for the buyer's solicitor to send a blank form to the seller's solicitor who rarely completes it but rather sends back a standard word processed version of the answers, usually adapted with only the identity of the lender and date of the charge to be discharged.

Some firms when acting for sellers submit the Completion Information and Undertakings form at the outset but that practice is not recommended by this Protocol. This is mainly because this is likely to result in the undertaking to discharge being given a long time in advance of actual completion when there is a greater possibility of the undertakings being given without full and current information as to the sums involved.

Buyer's and seller's solicitors must both consider the type of discharge that may be given by the lender. This is necessary because identification of the lender will be required in paper discharge cases and it may not be certain that a paper discharge will not be the eventual means of discharge regardless of the information provided before redemption takes place.

*Insurance*

The buyer's solicitor must advise the buyer of the necessity to commence insurance from the point of exchange as required by the Standard Conditions of Sale (SCS). The risks of this will need to be explained. The buyer will need to be advised of any requirements that their lender may have in relation to such insurance, including the perils indicated by the lender in its instructions and the minimum sum insured. It will be a useful exercise for the buyer to investigate the insurance terms available for the property they wish to buy well in advance of the likely exchange date. They may learn much about the property from the terms offered by a number of insurers. As flood risk cover becomes ever more important those insurers who have detailed information about flood risk and charge premiums that take this into account may be able to provide useful information to the buyer about the likely risks.

The contract regulates the position concerning who bears the cost of damage to the property if this occurs after exchange. The Protocol requires both the buyer and the seller to be advised by their solicitors about the position relating to insurance. Under the latest SCS (fifth edition) the risk of damage passes to the buyer at exchange.

Where the risk in the property has passed to the buyer then the contractual responsibility for any damage becomes that of the buyer. If he or she has insured adequately an insurance claim should produce the amount of the loss allowing completion to take place. However, it is highly unlikely that such funds will be available on completion. This may mean that the contract cannot be completed on the contractual completion date. This may expose the buyer to liability under the contract for late completion.

Even if the buyer has not insured, the SCS provide that the buyer must complete the transaction at the contract price. No allowance is to be made for the value of the damage. However, if the payment under the buyer's insurance policy is reduced because the property is also insured by the seller, the SCS provide that the purchase price will be reduced by the amount of any reduction. In practice it is likely that some sellers will continue to insure particularly where they have obligations to lenders in this regard.

If the property is damaged before completion, a buyer who is obtaining a mortgage will need the lender's consent to receive the advance. The value of the security may well be reduced and there is a risk that the mortgage offer will be withdrawn. In practice it is suggested that some lenders will be prepared to proceed once an insurance claim has been accepted and arrangements have been put in place for the insurance proceeds to be applied to the rebuilding.

*Preparation for completion*

In applications to lenders for redemption statements it is suggested that it is made clear to the lender that the seller and the seller's solicitor will be relying on their statement in order to give an undertaking. Asking lenders for statements for all and any charges (and giving all account numbers where possible) that they may have over the property is essential.

The buyer's solicitor needs to consider whether the Land Registry early completion policy will apply. He will need to consider the optimum time for carrying out an official search of the register with priority at the Land Registry. It is suggested this should not be too early, so as to leave the maximum priority period post-completion, and not so late that there is insufficient time for the seller's solicitor to provide any undertakings that will be required if the register has been changed.

The buyer's solicitor should supply the certificate on title and request the mortgage funds and other monies from the client required for completion in good time. Discuss with the buyer/borrower whether the mortgage monies should be requested to arrive the day before completion where the advance is sent by CHAPS, so that completion is not delayed whilst waiting for the mortgage advance to arrive. Advise the buyer/borrower that they may be charged an additional day's interest.

The day before completion endeavour to establish whether there is likely to be any delay and talk to clients if necessary.

### 4.5 Stage E: Completion

*General*

Particularly where clients are physically moving on the day of completion it is important to establish whether there is likely to be any delay in completion and if so to let them know.

In relation to undertakings see particularly the SRA warning card on undertakings.

See also 'Accepting undertakings on completion following the Court of Appeal decision in *Patel* v. *Daybells*' in the Appendices to the Law Society's *Conveyancing Handbook*.

There is no obligation to give or accept undertakings and it may be necessary in respect of certain loans and some lenders to consider making arrangements to have the charge discharged in advance of completion. This is particularly relevant in relation to second and third charges.

*Undertakings to discharge the seller's mortgage(s)*

The Protocol provides that the seller's solicitor should consider whether an undertaking to discharge the seller's mortgage is appropriate at all.

Having given an undertaking to discharge a mortgage the firm is obliged to pay all monies that might be required, even if these exceed the available sale proceeds.

There are risks involved in giving undertakings and steps should be taken to minimise these particularly in relation to situations where there may be 'negative equity' or where 'flexible' mortgage products are involved. Many developers will have given 'all monies' charges and the release of an individual property will necessitate specific agreement between the parties and a signed discharge.

'Offset' or 'flexible' accounts where a current account is linked to a mortgage account are relatively established in the residential mortgage market. Solicitors have used various different methods of establishing a 'fixed' redemption figure in these circumstances.

These have included:

- arranging to retain the proceeds of sale or an amount of funds pending the lender issuing the release;
- requesting the lender to 'freeze' the current account at the point of production of a redemption statement (which is only possible in practical terms where the borrower has access to other current account facilities);
- in circumstances where the bank will not freeze the account, asking the client who then agrees not to use the current account once the redemption statement has been supplied;
- asking the client to provide an additional sum to cover spending on this account prior to completion – some ask the lender for the maximum sum that could be withdrawn from the account in order to establish the maximum liability level – this is then the amount requested from the client.

All of these depend on the relationship the solicitor has with the client and his assessment of the matter generally.

Obviously there will be matters where solicitors are not able or willing to supply an undertaking on completion and these types of account may feature in a number of such cases. As solicitors should not underwrite the process if it is not reasonable for them to do so it may in some cases be necessary to advise clients to obtain bridging finance. As the process cannot assist consumers in these circumstances it is advisable to give notice of these issues as early as possible in the transaction.

Where an undertaking is to be given the form of the undertaking should be considered by both parties' solicitors.

The undertaking in respect of this discharge is often given under the provisions of the Law Society Code for Completion by Post (the Code). The Protocol requires the buyer's solicitor and the seller's solicitor to adopt the Code without variation unless instructions are given by the client, which are specific to the needs of the individual transaction. Standard exclusions of liability for obligations arising under the Code are a breach of the Protocol.

Where the buyer's lender is separately represented and is not represented by the buyer's solicitor it will be necessary to check what form of undertaking for discharge will be required by the solicitor acting for the buyer's lender as well as by the solicitor acting for the buyer. The solicitor acting for the buyer's lender may require that the undertaking be provided directly to them rather than to the buyer's solicitor.

By adopting the Code the seller's solicitor is under an obligation to send the signed transfer and other agreed documents on the day of completion to the buyer's solicitor.

The seller's solicitor should check that the seller agrees the redemption statement, particularly in relation to penalty or early redemption payments, and advise the seller about mortgage payments that fall due to be paid prior to the completion date.

APPENDIX A

**4.6 Stage F: Post-completion**

After completion inform the clients and as necessary the other party's solicitor and the estate agent (for keys) that it has taken place. The seller's solicitor should send the completion documents to the buyer's solicitor under the Code if used. The buyer's solicitor should then file the SDLT return (the client having previously agreed and signed a hard copy). Remember it is the tax return of the client.

Following completion the buyer's solicitor must apply to register the transactions within the priority period of the official search.

The seller's solicitor should provide the buyer's solicitor with the discharge or confirmation that it has been remitted promptly. If the discharge is to take place by form DS1 this needs to be supplied to the buyer's solicitor as soon as it is received. If the lender has discharged any registered charge by electronic means the seller's solicitor should notify the buyer's solicitor when confirmation is received from the lender. If none is received, the Protocol requires the seller's solicitor to contact the lender to obtain such confirmation. When the discharge has been remitted or supplied and the buyer is confident that this has taken place he can confirm that the undertaking in that respect has been discharged.

There can, as solicitors will be only too well aware, be delays in obtaining evidence of the discharge of the existing charge from some lenders. This may mean the Land Registry will implement its 'early completion' policy. This allows registration of the purchase and new mortgage to take place even if no notification or documentation relating to the discharged mortgage has been received by the Land Registry. It is important to apply for registration within the priority period of the search to retain the protection of the search rather than wait for evidence of discharge. Remember that it is not possible to maintain priority by 'renewing' searches. Priority searches cannot be 'renewed'. It is just fortuitous if no other application has been lodged in the meantime. This is the case each time an application is made to 'renew' a priority search. Were all lenders to provide evidence of discharge promptly these issues would largely disappear.

If there is a restriction in the seller's charge that prevents other dispositions being registered, the buyer's solicitor should request that the Land Registry grant an extension of the time for lodging the discharge to prevent rejection of the application at a later date. Such an extension can usually be requested when the Land Registry raises requisitions.

When the buyer's solicitor receives the title information document (TID) from the Land Registry showing the title of the buyer to the property and the lender's interest they should check its contents including the address(es) for service. A copy should be sent to the buyer, who should be reminded of the benefits of keeping the address(es) for service up to date. The lender should be advised of registration. Lenders have different requirements as to what documents they require following completion and these will normally be set out in Part 2 of the CML Lenders' Handbook.

*After completion*

Post-completion the obligation to provide a discharge continues. Even if the discharge is provided electronically the seller's solicitor should tell the buyer's solicitor when they are notified by the lender that the discharge has been given. The buyer's solicitor should not wait for evidence of the discharge before applying for registration in an attempt to avoid the application of the early completion procedure. This creates too much risk for the buyer's solicitor. It is not possible to be certain of preserving priority. If another application is made during the currency of the buyer's search by a third party the buyer's solicitor's subsequent search result will be subject to this intervening application. The fact that one might be lucky enough to obtain a further clear search with a new period of priority is not the basis of good practice.

*Separate representation*

There are sections in Protocol about separate representation. Many lenders have reduced numbers on their panels to such an extent that some degree of separate representation has been introduced by lenders. The buyer's solicitor should make arrangements as soon as possible to ascertain precisely what will be required by the lender's solicitor and if any change in procedure is required, for example, an undertaking for discharge directly from the seller's solicitor to the lender's solicitor, this should be dealt with as soon as reasonably possible in order to expedite matters, post-exchange.

## 5. PROTOCOL MATERIALS

### 5.1 Standard Conditions of Sale (fifth edition)

When sending out the contract bundle, the seller's solicitor should use the latest edition of the Standard Conditions of Sale and should not add further additional special conditions unless they are necessary to accord with current law or specific and informed instructions have been given by the seller that inclusion of such clauses are necessary and are required for the purposes of a particular transaction.

This obligation is designed to stop the multitude of unnecessary special conditions which increase workloads and can militate against co-operation.

Because buyers are often also sellers and sellers are often also buyers the Standard Conditions are designed to provide a fair balance between the seller and the buyer.

See Explanatory Notes to the Standard Conditions of Sale (fifth edition) (Law Society and Solicitors Law Stationery Society, 2011).

Whilst the Protocol is a form of 'preferred practice' and recommends the use of the Standard Conditions of Sale without amendment where appropriate, the solicitor must use his knowledge and judgement and act in the best interests of the client. It is hoped, however, that the Standard Conditions of Sale (fifth edition) will be used with little or no amendment save where the law or clients' instructions require.

### 5.2 Enquiry forms

The forms that continue in use following the abolition of the HIPs legislation are set out below.

- Property Information Form (TA6)
  This form was expanded from the previous preliminary enquiry form both to accommodate HIPs requirements and to raise enquiries commonly requested by buyers. Even though the questions requested to be asked by buyers are not strictly necessary for the production of the form of Certificate of Title set out in rule 3 of the Solicitors' Code of Conduct 2007 they can be useful to buyers generally. There are difficult areas here in the context of caveat emptor but because many sellers are also buyers the Law Society aims to balance the respective rights of buyers and sellers in the framing of these enquiries.
- Leasehold Information Form (TA7)
- New Home Information Form (TA8)
- Fittings and Contents Form (TA10)
  This form sets out those items that are or are not to be included in the sale. It is possible for further sums to be charged for items in addition to the purchase price. This form is to make the position regarding items to be included in the sale clear to buyers and sellers.

APPENDIX A

Another aspect of matters relating to these items is the reasonableness of the price for stamp duty land tax purposes. To agree a figure that is not just and reasonable for the purposes of saving stamp duty land tax is a criminal offence: **www.hmrc.gov.uk/manuals/sdltmanual/sdltm04010.htm**.
- Completion Arrangements and Undertakings (TA13)
  This form has been changed to reflect practice.

### 5.3 Exchange formulae

The exchange formulae remain A, B and C and these have not changed.

It has always been necessary to record an agreed memorandum of the details of the exchange and any agreed variation of the formula used at the time of the exchange and to retain this in the file. Agreed variations should also be confirmed in writing to the other side. The serious risks of exchanging contracts without a deposit or with a deposit being 'held to order' should be explained to and accepted by the seller client.

The new version of the Standard Conditions of Sale (fifth edition) makes provision for a record of the exchange on the front sheet of the contract itself although it does not form part of the contract. Such a record can be extremely important if any question about the exchange were raised subsequently.

As those who effect the exchange will bind their firms or other organisations to the undertakings in the formula used, solicitors should carefully consider who is authorised to effect exchange under the formulae and ensure that use of the procedure is restricted to them. They may also want to ascertain the identity and status of the person with whom they are effecting the exchange. Since professional undertakings form the basis of the formulae they are only recommended for use between solicitors and licensed conveyancers.

### 5.4 Code for Completion by Post

The Law Society Code for Completion by Post (the Code) provides a voluntary procedure for postal rather than physical completion for residential transactions. It outlines a clear structure for the completion process and clear obligations of sellers' and buyers' solicitors.

The objective of the Code is to provide solicitors with a convenient means for completion on an agency basis when a representative of the buyer's solicitor is not attending at the office of the seller's solicitor.

It may also be used by licensed conveyancers.

It contains important professional obligations and practices will need to ensure that it is dealt with at an appropriate level of seniority within the practice.

Solicitors adopting the Code must be satisfied that its adoption will not be contrary to the interests of their client. When adopted, the Code applies without variation unless otherwise agreed.

To adopt the Code both parties must agree in writing to use the Code to complete a specific transaction except if they have already made it clear that they will be using the Protocol in which case the Code is automatically implied.

The Code has been updated and revised and solicitors are advised to take note of the contents of the revised Code and the notes to the Code.

## 6. REVIEW OF CONTENT AND CONTACT INFORMATION

Users of the Protocol and supporting documentation are encouraged to provide information as to its operation and content. The Protocol and supporting documentation will be updated regularly.

**How to contact us**

For queries in relation to membership and other matters relating to CQS contact **CQS@lawsociety.org.uk** or 0207 316 5550.

For queries or comments on the Protocol, the Standard Conditions of Sale, the TA forms, the formulae, the Code or these notes contact **protocolfeedback@lawsociety.org.uk**.

# APPENDIX B(I)

# TA6 Property information form

## Property Information Form (2nd edition) — TA6

**Address of the property**

Postcode ☐☐☐☐☐☐☐

**Full names of the seller**

**Seller's solicitor**
Name of solicitors firm

Address

Email

Reference number

**About this form**

This form is completed by the seller to supply the detailed information and documents which may be relied upon for the conveyancing process.

**Definitions**

- 'Seller' means all sellers together where the property is owned by more than one person
- 'Buyer' means all buyers together where the property is being bought by more than one person
- 'Property' includes all buildings and land within its boundaries

The Law Society

© Law Society 2009. Reproduced with the assistance of Oyez Professional Services Limited.

# TA6 PROPERTY INFORMATION FORM

**Instructions to the seller**

The answers should be prepared by the person or persons who are named as owner on the deeds or Land Registry title or by the owner's legal representative(s) if selling under a power of attorney or grant of probate or representation. If there is more than one seller, you should prepare the answers together.

It is very important that your answers are accurate. If you give incorrect or incomplete information to the buyer (on this form or otherwise, in writing or in conversation, whether through your estate agent or solicitor or directly to the buyer), the buyer may make a claim for compensation from you or refuse to complete the purchase.

You should answer the questions based upon information known to you (or, in the case of legal representatives, you or the owner). You are not expected to have expert knowledge of legal or technical matters.

If you do not know the answer to any question, you must say so. If you are unsure of the meaning of any questions or answers, please ask your solicitor. This form can be completed in full, in part or not at all. Omissions or delay in providing some information may delay the sale.

If you later become aware of any information which would alter any replies you have given, you must inform your solicitor immediately. This is as important as giving the right answers in the first place. Do not change any arrangements concerning the property with anyone (such as a tenant or neighbour) without first consulting your solicitor.

Please give your solicitor any letters, agreements or other papers which help answer the questions. If you are aware of any which you are not supplying with the answers, tell your solicitor. Some of the questions provide 'Lost' as an answer. If you indicate that some of the documentation is lost you may need to obtain copies at your own expense. Also pass to your solicitor any notices you have received concerning the property and any which arrive at any time before completion of the sale.

Please also complete *TA10 Fittings and Contents Form*. This may form part of the contract between you and the buyer and must be completed accurately.

**Instructions to the buyer**

If the seller gives you, separately from this form, any information concerning the property (in writing or in conversation, whether through an estate agent or solicitor or directly to you) on which you wish to rely when buying the property, you should tell your solicitor so that it can be recorded in the contract.

You should carefully check *TA10 Fittings and Contents Form*. This may form part of the contract between you and the seller.

APPENDIX B(I)

## 1 Boundaries and boundary features (fences, walls, hedges, ditches or similar)

1.1 Looking towards the property from the road, who owns or accepts responsibility to maintain or repair the boundary features:

(a) on the left?
☐ Seller    ☐ Neighbour
☐ Shared    ☐ Not known

(b) on the right?
☐ Seller    ☐ Neighbour
☐ Shared    ☐ Not known

(c) at the rear?
☐ Seller    ☐ Neighbour
☐ Shared    ☐ Not known

(d) at the front?
☐ Seller    ☐ Neighbour
☐ Shared    ☐ Not known

1.2 Has any boundary feature been moved in the last 20 years? If Yes, please give details:
☐ Yes    ☐ No

1.3 During the seller's ownership, has any land previously forming part of the property been sold or has any adjacent property been purchased? If Yes, please give details:
☐ Yes    ☐ No

1.4 Does any part of the property or any building on the property overhang, or project under, the boundary of the neighbouring property or road? If Yes, please give details:
☐ Yes    ☐ No

## 2 Disputes and complaints

2.1 Have there been or are there any disputes or complaints regarding this property or a property nearby? If Yes, please give details:
☐ Yes    ☐ No

**TA6 PROPERTY INFORMATION FORM**

2.2 Does the seller know of anything which might lead to a dispute about the property or a property nearby? If Yes, please give details:   ☐ Yes   ☐ No

## 3 Notices and proposals

3.1 Have any notices or correspondence been received or sent (e.g. from or to a neighbour, council or government department), or any negotiations or discussions taken place, which affect the property or a property nearby? If Yes, please give details:   ☐ Yes   ☐ No

3.2 Is the seller aware of any proposals to develop property or land nearby, or of any proposals to make alterations to buildings nearby? If Yes, please give details:   ☐ Yes   ☐ No

## 4 Alterations, planning and building control

**Note:** All relevant approvals and supporting paperwork referred to in section 4 of this form, such as listed building consents, planning permissions, building regulations consents and completion certificates must be provided prior to exchange of contracts. Some works will require notification to the local authority either directly or through a Competent Persons Scheme.

4.1 Has the property been used otherwise than as a private home at any time during the last 10 years? If Yes, please give details:   ☐ Yes   ☐ No   ☐ Not known

APPENDIX B(I)

4.2 Have any of the following changes been made to the whole or any part of the property (including the garden)? If Yes, in what year were the changes made?

(a) Building works — ☐ Yes ☐ No [ ] Year

(b) Change of use (e.g. from a shop to a residence) — ☐ Yes ☐ No [ ] Year

(c) Conversion (e.g. loft or garage conversion) — ☐ Yes ☐ No [ ] Year

(d) Electrical work since 1 January 2005 — ☐ Yes ☐ No [ ] Year

(e) Installation of a solar panel — ☐ Yes ☐ No [ ] Year

(f) Installation of air conditioning — ☒ Yes ☐ No [ ] Year

(g) Installation of a satellite dish (above the roof line only) — ☒ Yes ☐ No [ ] Year

(h) Installation of replacement windows, roof windows, roof lights, glazed doors since 1 April 2002 — ☒ Yes ☐ No [ ] Year

(i) Installation of central heating system or renewable energy heating system, or other water or plumbing system changes, since 1 April 2005 — ☐ Yes ☐ No [ ] Year

4.3 Are any of the works disclosed in 4.2 above unfinished? ☐ Yes ☐ No
If Yes, please give details:

4.4 Are there any planning or building control issues to resolve? ☐ Yes ☐ No
If Yes, please give details:

**Conservatory**

4.5 Does the property include a conservatory? If Yes: ☐ Yes ☐ No

(a) In what year was it built? [ ] Year ☐ Not known

(b) Does it have building regulations approval? If Yes, please supply a copy.
☐ Yes ☐ No
☐ Not known ☐ Enclosed
☐ To follow ☐ Lost

# TA6 PROPERTY INFORMATION FORM

## 5 Guarantees and warranties

**Note:** All available guarantees, warranties and supporting paperwork should be provided before exchange of contracts.

5.1 Does the property benefit from any of the following guarantees or warranties? If Yes, please supply a copy.

| | | |
|---|---|---|
| (a) New home warranty (e.g. NHBC or similar) | ☐ Yes ☐ Enclosed | ☐ No ☐ To follow |
| (b) Damp proofing | ☐ Yes ☐ Enclosed | ☐ No ☐ To follow |
| (c) Timber treatment | ☐ Yes ☐ Enclosed | ☐ No ☐ To follow |
| (d) Glazing, roof lights, roof windows or glazed doors | ☐ Yes ☐ Enclosed | ☐ No ☐ To follow |
| (e) Electrical work | ☐ Yes ☐ Enclosed | ☐ No ☐ To follow |
| (f) Roofing | ☐ Yes ☐ Enclosed | ☐ No ☐ To follow |
| (g) Central heating | ☐ Yes ☐ Enclosed | ☐ No ☐ To follow |
| (h) Underpinning | ☐ Yes ☐ Enclosed | ☐ No ☐ To follow |
| (i) Other (please state): | ☐ Enclosed | ☐ To follow |

5.2 Have any claims been made under any of these guarantees or warranties? If Yes, please give details:   ☐ Yes   ☐ No

## 6 Council tax

**Note:** If any alterations or improvements have been made since the property was last valued for council tax, the sale of the property may trigger a revaluation. This may mean that following completion of the sale, the property may be put into a higher council tax band. For more information, see the Valuation Office website at **www.voa.gov.uk**

6.1 Which council tax band is the property in?   Band (A–H)

6.2 How much is payable this year?   £

APPENDIX B(I)

### 7 Environmental matters

**Note:** 'Property' includes all buildings and land within its boundaries.

7.1 Has the property suffered from flooding? If Yes, please give details:   ☐ Yes   ☐ No

**Note:** Flooding may take a variety of forms: it may be seasonal or irregular or simply a one off occurrence.

7.2 Has a Radon test been carried out on the property? If Yes:   ☐ Yes   ☐ No
   ☐ Not known

(a) please supply a copy of the report   ☐ Enclosed   ☐ To follow
   ☐ Lost

(b) was the test result below the 'recommended action level'?   ☐ Yes   ☐ No

**Note:** Radon is a naturally occurring inert radioactive gas found in the ground. Some parts of England and Wales are more adversely affected by it than others.

7.3 Were any remedial measures undertaken on construction to reduce Radon gas levels in the property?   ☐ Yes   ☐ No
   ☐ Not known

**Note:** Remedial action is advised for properties with a test result above the 'recommended action level'. For more information, see **www.hpa.org.uk**.

7.4 Please supply a copy of the Energy Performance Certificate (EPC) for the property.   ☐ Enclosed   ☐ To follow
   ☐ Already supplied

7.5 For new homes built under building regulations approval obtained under applications dated on or after 1 May 2008, please supply a copy of the Sustainability Certificate or the Nil-rated Certificate as appropriate.   ☐ Enclosed
   ☐ Already supplied
   ☐ Not applicable

### 8 Formal and informal arrangements

**Note:** Formal and informal arrangements may relate to access or shared use, for example.

8.1 Does ownership of the property carry a responsibility to contribute towards the cost of any jointly used services, such as maintenance of a private road, a shared driveway, a boundary or drain? If Yes, please give details:   ☐ Yes   ☐ No

# TA6 PROPERTY INFORMATION FORM

**8.2** Does the property benefit from any formal or informal arrangements over any neighbouring property? If Yes, please give details:  ☐ Yes  ☐ No

**8.3** Are there any formal or informal arrangements which someone else has over the property? If Yes, please give details:  ☐ Yes  ☐ No

**8.4** Has anyone taken steps to prevent access to the property, or to complain about or demand payment for access to the property? If Yes, please give details:  ☐ Yes  ☐ No

## 9 Other charges

**Note:** If the property is leasehold, details of lease expenses such as service charges and ground rent should be set out on the separate *TA7 Leasehold Information Form*.

**9.1** Does the seller ever have to pay for the use of the property (excluding any payments already stated in this form, such as council tax, utility charges, etc)? If Yes, please give details:  ☐ Yes  ☐ No

## 10 Occupiers

**10.1** Does the seller live at the property?  ☐ Yes  ☐ No

**10.2** Does anyone else, aged 17 or over, live at the property?  ☐ Yes  ☐ No

If **No** to question 10.2, please continue to section 11 'Transaction information' and do not answer 10.3–10.5 below.

APPENDIX B(I)

**10.3** Please give the full names of any occupiers aged 17 or over:

**10.4** Are any of the occupiers, aged 17 or over, tenants or lodgers? ☐ Yes ☐ No

**10.5** Is the property being sold with vacant possession? ☐ Yes ☐ No
If Yes, have all the occupiers aged 17 or over:

(a) agreed to leave prior to completion? ☐ Yes ☐ No

(b) agreed to sign the sale contract? If No, please supply other evidence that the property will be vacant on completion. ☐ Yes ☐ No
☐ Enclosed ☐ To follow

## 11 Transaction information

**11.1** Is the sale dependent on the seller buying another property? ☐ Yes ☐ No
If Yes, please give details of the stage that negotiations have reached:

**11.2** Does the seller have any special requirements about a moving date? If Yes, please give details: ☐ Yes ☐ No

**11.3** Does the seller expect to use the deposit received on a related purchase? ☐ Yes ☐ No

**11.4** Does the sale price exceed the amount necessary to repay all charges secured on the property? ☐ Yes ☐ No

## 12 Services

**Note:** If the seller does not have a certificate requested below this can be obtained from the relevant Competent Persons Scheme. Schemes authorised by the Department for Communities and Local Government are listed on its website **www.communities.gov.uk**

# TA6 PROPERTY INFORMATION FORM

### Electricity

**12.1** Has the electrical system been tested and approved?
If Yes, please supply a copy of the test certificate or results.
☐ Yes ☐ No
☐ Not known
☐ Enclosed ☐ To follow

### Central heating

**12.2** Is there a central heating system at the property? If Yes: ☐ Yes ☐ No

(a) What type of system is it (e.g. mains gas, liquid gas, oil, electricity, etc)? _____

(b) When was the heating system installed? If on or after 1 April 2005 please supply a copy of the 'completion certificate' (or the 'exceptional circumstances' form) and a completed Benchmark Scheme log book.
_____ Date
☐ Not known
☐ Enclosed ☐ To follow

(c) Is the heating system in good working order? ☐ Yes ☐ No

(d) In what year was the heating system last serviced/maintained? _____ Year ☐ Not known

### Drainage and sewerage

**12.3** Is the property connected to mains surface water drainage? ☐ Yes ☐ No

**12.4** Is sewerage for the property provided by a septic tank or cesspool? ☐ Yes ☐ No

**If No to question 12.4, please continue to section 13 'Connection to utilities and services' and do not answer 12.5–12.8 below.**

**12.5** Is the use of the septic tank or cesspool shared with other properties? If Yes, how many properties share the system?
☐ Yes ☐ No
_____ Properties sharing

**12.6** In what year was the system last emptied? _____ Year

**12.7** In what year was the system installed? If installed since 1 January 1991 please supply copies of the relevant building regulations and Environment Agency consents.
_____ Year ☐ Not known
☐ Enclosed ☐ To follow
☐ Lost

**12.8** Is any part of the septic tank or cesspool, or the access to it, outside the boundary of the property? If Yes, please supply a plan showing the location of the septic tank or cesspool and how access is obtained.
☐ Yes ☐ No
☐ Enclosed ☐ To follow

APPENDIX B(I)

## 13 Connection to utilities and services

**13.1** Please mark the Yes or No boxes to show which of the following utilities and services are connected to the property and give details of any providers.

| Mains electricity ☐ Yes ☐ No | Mains gas ☐ Yes ☐ No |
|---|---|
| Provider's name | Provider's name |
| Provider's telephone number | Provider's telephone number |
| Location of meter | Location of meter |

| Mains water ☐ Yes ☐ No | Mains sewerage ☐ Yes ☐ No |
|---|---|
| Provider's name | Provider's name |
| Provider's telephone number | Provider's telephone number |
| Location of stop cock | Location of meter, if any |
| Location of meter, if any | |

| Telephone ☐ Yes ☐ No | Cable ☐ Yes ☐ No |
|---|---|
| Provider's name | Provider's name |
| Provider's telephone number | Provider's telephone number |

*SPECIMEN*

© Law Society 2009 — Property Information Form TA6

TA6 PROPERTY INFORMATION FORM

| Satellite | ☐ Yes ☐ No | Broadband | ☐ Yes ☐ No |
|---|---|---|---|
| Provider's name | | Provider's name | |
| Provider's telephone number | | Provider's telephone number | |

Signed: ........................................................... Dated: ................................

Each seller should sign this form.

# APPENDIX B(II)

# TA7 Leasehold information form

## Leasehold Information Form (2nd edition) — TA7

**Address of the property**

Postcode ☐☐☐☐☐☐☐

**Full names of the seller**

**Seller's solicitor**

Name of solicitors firm

Address

Email

Reference number

**Definitions**
- 'Seller' means all sellers together where the property is owned by more than one person
- 'Buyer' means all buyers together where the property is being bought by more than one person
- 'Property' means the leasehold property being sold
- 'Building' means the building containing the property
- 'Neighbour' means those occupying flats in the building

**Instructions to the seller**

The seller should provide all relevant documentation relating to the lease when they return this completed form to their solicitor. This may include documents given to the seller when they purchased the property, or documents subsequently given to the seller by those managing the property.

**Instructions to the seller and the buyer**

Please read the notes on *TA6 Property Information Form*

The Law Society — www.lawsociety.org.uk

© Law Society 2009. Reproduced with the assistance of Oyez Professional Services Limited.

# TA7 LEASEHOLD INFORMATION FORM

## 1 The property

**1.1** What type of leasehold property does the seller own? ('Flat' includes maisonette and apartment).
- ☐ Flat
- ☐ Shared ownership
- ☐ Long leasehold house

**1.2** Does the seller pay rent for the property? If Yes:  ☐ Yes  ☐ No

(a) How much is the current yearly rent? £ _____

(b) How regularly is the rent paid (e.g. yearly)? _____ Payments

## 2 Relevant documents

**2.1** Please supply a copy of:

(a) the lease and any supplemental deeds
- ☐ Enclosed  ☐ To follow
- ☐ Already supplied

(b) any regulations made by the landlord or by the tenants' management company additional to those in the lease
- ☐ Enclosed  ☐ To follow
- ☐ Not applicable

**2.2** Please supply a copy of any correspondence from the landlord, the management company and the managing agent.
- ☐ Enclosed  ☐ To follow

**2.3** Please supply a copy of any invoices or demands and any statements and receipts for the payment of:

(a) maintenance or service charges for the last three years
- ☐ Enclosed  ☐ To follow
- ☐ Not applicable

(b) ground rent for the last three years
- ☐ Enclosed  ☐ To follow
- ☐ Not applicable

**2.4** Please supply a copy of the buildings insurance policy:

(a) arranged by the seller and a receipt for payment of the last premium, **or**
- ☐ Enclosed  ☐ To follow

(b) arranged by the landlord or management company and the schedule for the current year
- ☐ Enclosed  ☐ To follow

**2.5** Have the tenants formed a management company to manage the building? If Yes, please supply a copy of:  ☐ Yes  ☐ No

(a) the Memorandum and Articles of Association
- ☐ Enclosed  ☐ To follow

(b) the share or membership certificate
- ☐ Enclosed  ☐ To follow

(c) the company accounts for the past three years
- ☐ Enclosed  ☐ To follow

APPENDIX B(II)

## 3 Management of the building

**3.1** Does the landlord employ a managing agent to collect rent or manage the building? ☐ Yes ☐ No

**3.2** Has any management company formed by the tenants been dissolved or struck off the register at Companies House? ☐ Yes ☐ No ☐ Not known

**3.3** Do the tenants pass day to day responsibility for the management of the building to managing agents? ☐ Yes ☐ No

## 4 Contact details

**4.1** Please supply contact details for the following, where appropriate. (The landlord may be, for example, a private individual, a housing association, or a management company owned by the residents. A managing agent may be employed by the landlord or by the tenants' management company to collect the rent and/or manage the building.)

|  | **Landlord** | **Managing agent contracted by the landlord** |
|---|---|---|
| Name | | |
| Address | | |
| Tel | | |
| Email | | |

|  | **Managing agent contracted by the tenants' management company** |
|---|---|
| Name | |
| Address | |
| Tel | |
| Email | |

© Law Society 2009 — Leasehold Information Form TA7

## TA7 LEASEHOLD INFORMATION FORM

### 5 Maintenance and service charges

**5.1** Who is responsible for arranging the buildings insurance on the property?
☐ Seller
☐ Management company
☐ Landlord

**5.2** In what year was the outside of the building last decorated?
[ ] Year ☐ Not known

**5.3** In what year were any internal communal parts last decorated?
[ ] Year ☐ Not known

**5.4** Does the seller contribute to the cost of maintaining the building?
☐ Yes ☐ No

**If No to question 5.4, please continue to section 6 'Notices' and do not answer questions 5.5–5.9 below.**

**5.5** Does the seller know of any expense (e.g. the cost of redecoration of outside or communal areas not usually incurred annually) likely to be shown in the service charge accounts within the next three years? If Yes, please give details:
☐ Yes ☐ No

**5.6** Does the seller know of any problems in the last three years regarding the level of service charges or with the management? If Yes, please give details:
☐ Yes ☐ No

**5.7** Has the seller challenged the service charge or any expense in the last three years? If Yes, please give details:
☐ Yes ☐ No

**5.8** Is the seller aware of any difficulties encountered in collecting the service charges from other flat owners? If Yes, please give details:
☐ Yes ☐ No

© Law Society 2009

Leasehold Information Form TA7

APPENDIX B(II)

**5.9** Does the seller owe any service charges, rent, insurance premium or other financial contribution? If Yes, please give details:

☐ Yes ☐ No

## 6 Notices

**Note:** A notice may be in a printed form or in the form of a letter.

**6.1** Has the seller received a notice that the landlord wants to sell the building? If Yes, please supply a copy.

☐ Yes ☐ No
☐ Enclosed ☐ To follow
☐ Lost

**6.2** Has the seller received any other notice about the building, its use, its condition or its repair and maintenance? If Yes, please supply a copy.

☐ Yes ☐ No
☐ Enclosed ☐ To follow
☐ Lost

## 7 Consents

**Note:** A consent may be given in a formal document, a letter or orally.

**7.1** Is the seller aware of any changes in the terms of the lease or of the landlord giving any consents under the lease? If Yes, please supply a copy or, if not in writing, please give details:

☐ Yes ☐ No
☐ Enclosed ☐ To follow
☐ Lost

## 8 Complaints

**8.1** Has the seller received any complaint from the landlord, the management company or any neighbour about anything the seller has or has not done? If Yes, please give details:

☐ Yes ☐ No

TA7 LEASEHOLD INFORMATION FORM

8.2 Has the seller complained or had cause to complain to or about the landlord, the management company, or any neighbour? If Yes, please give details:  ☐ Yes   ☐ No

## 9 Alterations

9.1 Is the seller aware of any alterations having been made to the property since the lease was originally granted?  ☐ Yes   ☐ No

**If No, please go to section 10 'Enfranchisement' and do not answer 9.2 and 9.3 below.**

9.2 Please give details of these alterations:

9.3 Was the landlord's consent for the alterations obtained? If Yes, please supply a copy.
☐ Yes   ☐ No
☐ Not known   ☐ Not required
☐ Enclosed   ☐ To follow

## 10 Enfranchisement

**Note:** 'Enfranchisement' is the right of a tenant to purchase the freehold from their landlord and the right of the tenant to extend the term of the lease.

10.1 Has the seller owned the property for at least two years?  ☐ Yes   ☐ No

10.2 Has the seller served on the landlord a formal notice stating the seller's wish to buy the freehold or be granted an extended lease? If Yes, please supply a copy.
☐ Yes   ☐ No
☐ Enclosed   ☐ To follow
☐ Lost

10.3 Is the seller aware of the service of any notice relating to the possible collective purchase of the freehold of the building or part of it by a group of tenants? If Yes, please supply a copy.
☐ Yes   ☐ No
☐ Enclosed   ☐ To follow
☐ Lost

10.4 Is the seller aware of any response to a notice disclosed in replies to 10.2 and 10.3 above? If Yes, please supply a copy.
☐ Yes   ☐ No
☐ Enclosed   ☐ To follow
☐ Lost

Signed: ...................................................................   Dated: ................................

Each seller should sign this form.

# APPENDIX B(III)

# TA8 New home information form

## New home information form

Document date [ ][ ]/[ ][ ]/[ ][ ][ ][ ]

Address or proposed address of the property

Postcode [ ][ ][ ][ ][ ][ ][ ]  Plot number [            ]

This form should be completed and read in conjunction with the explanatory notes available separately

### 1 For all properties

1. Please confirm that an Energy Performance Certificate will be provided as soon as the property is physically complete.  ☐ Yes

2. Please state the estimated dates for:
   (a) physical completion of the property
   (b) certification that the property is fit for occupation

3. Is the warranty of any professional consultant available in relation to the monitoring of the construction or conversion of the property?  ☐ Yes  ☐ No
   If Yes, please give details:

4. Are all easements necessary for the enjoyment of the property fully available?  ☐ Yes  ☐ No
   If No, please give details:

Page 1 of 6
www.hips.lawsociety.org.uk
The Law Society
TA8
© Law Society 2007
TA8/1

© Law Society 2007. Reproduced with the assistance of Oyez Professional Services Limited.

TA8 NEW HOME INFORMATION FORM

5. Is there any road or sewer abutting or serving the property that has not been adopted?   ☐ Yes  ☐ No  ☐ Enclosed  ☐ To follow

   If Yes, please give details and supply a copy of any adoption agreement and bond:

6. Please specify which of the following services are or will be connected to or at the property.

   If the supplies will be connected in the future, please also give the proposed dates of connection if known.

| | Connected |
|---|---|
| Electricity | ☐ Yes  ☐ N/A  ☐ Will be ☐☐/☐☐/☐☐ |
| Gas | ☐ Yes  ☐ N/A  ☐ Will be ☐☐/☐☐/☐☐ |
| Mains water | ☐ Yes  ☐ N/A  ☐ Will be ☐☐/☐☐/☐☐ |
| Private drains | ☐ Yes  ☐ N/A  ☐ Will be ☐☐/☐☐/☐☐ |
| Private water | ☐ Yes  ☐ N/A  ☐ Will be ☐☐/☐☐/☐☐ |
| Septic tank/Cesspit | ☐ Yes  ☐ N/A  ☐ Will be ☐☐/☐☐/☐☐ |
| Telephone | ☐ Yes  ☐ N/A  ☐ Will be ☐☐/☐☐/☐☐ |

APPENDIX B(III)

7. Which if any of the following services at the property are fully operational?

| | | | |
|---|---|---|---|
| Boiler | ☐ Yes | ☐ No | ☐ N/A |
| Space heating | ☐ Yes | ☐ No | ☐ N/A |
| Water heating | ☐ Yes | ☐ No | ☐ N/A |
| Lift | ☐ Yes | ☐ No | ☐ N/A |

If No, for any of these services, please give details:

8. Please provide copies of any guarantees that are available or will be available at completion in relation to the following:

| | | | |
|---|---|---|---|
| Damp | ☐ Yes ☐ No | ☐ Enclosed | ☐ To follow |
| Double glazing, roof lights, roof windows, glazed doors | ☐ Yes ☐ No | ☐ Enclosed | ☐ To follow |
| Electrical appliances | ☐ Yes ☐ No | ☐ Enclosed | ☐ To follow |
| Electrical work | ☐ Yes ☐ No | ☐ Enclosed | ☐ To follow |
| Heating systems | ☐ Yes ☐ No | ☐ Enclosed | ☐ To follow |
| Hot water systems | ☐ Yes ☐ No | ☐ Enclosed | ☐ To follow |
| New home warranty | ☐ Yes ☐ No | ☐ Enclosed | ☐ To follow |
| Timber infestation | ☐ Yes ☐ No | ☐ Enclosed | ☐ To follow |
| Roofing | ☐ Yes ☐ No | ☐ Enclosed | ☐ To follow |
| Ventilation systems | ☐ Yes ☐ No | ☐ Enclosed | ☐ To follow |

*New home information form* **TA8**
TA8/3

9. Has any application been made for street naming and numbering and for allocation of a postcode?

If Yes, please provide copies of responses.

☐ Yes  ☐ No  ☐ Enclosed
☐ To follow

10. Please confirm whether the property has:

   (a) been inspected by the valuation officer

   ☐ Yes  ☐ No

   If No, please give details:

   **or**

   (b) entered on the valuation list for council tax

   ☐ Yes  ☐ No

   If No, please give details:

11. Please state the council tax valuation band for the property and the amount of the annual payment.

   Band A - H [         ]
   Amount £ [         ] yearly

12. Has the billing authority issued any completion notice in respect of the property?

   ☐ Yes  ☐ No

   If No, please give details:

## 2  Leasehold

1. Please provide a copy of any budget or estimate for payments in the 12 months after completion in respect of service and maintenance charges, insurance and any reserve fund.

   ☐ Enclosed  ☐ To follow

2. Have managing agents been appointed or is it intended that managing agents will be appointed?

   ☐ Yes  ☐ No
   ☐ To be appointed

   If Yes, or to be appointed, please give contact details including name, address, telephone number, and email:

APPENDIX B(III)

3. Has any management company been formed in respect of which any shares are to be issued to the buyer or any other occupier of a flat within the development? ☐ Yes ☐ No

   If Yes, please give details:

4. Are there any communal or shared areas or other parts of the development that will remain to be completed after completion of the property? ☐ Yes ☐ No

   If Yes, please give details:

5. Is there any contract or arrangement for the sale of the freehold reversion? ☐ Yes ☐ No

   If Yes, please give details:

6. Are any negotiations in progress for the sale of the freehold reversion? ☐ Yes ☐ No

   If Yes, please give details:

## 3 Commonhold

1. Please provide a copy of any budget or estimate for the commonhold assessment payments in the 12 months after completion in respect of maintenance charges, insurance and any reserve fund. ☐ Enclosed ☐ To follow

2. Please provide the contact details of the commonhold association:

# TA8 NEW HOME INFORMATION FORM

3. Have managing agents been appointed or is it intended that managing agents will be appointed? ☐ Yes ☐ No ☐ To be appointed

   If Yes, or to be appointed, please give contact details including name, address, telephone number, and email:

4. How many unit holders will there be?

5. Are there any communal or shared areas or other parts of the development that will remain to be completed after completion of the property? ☐ Yes ☐ No

   If Yes, please give details:

6. When will the transfer of the common parts take place? ☐☐/☐☐/☐☐

7. Does the commonhold community statement give 'development rights'? ☐ Yes ☐ No

   If Yes, please give details:

The information in this form has been given by:

Name

# APPENDIX B(IV)

# TA10 Fittings and contents form

**Fittings and Contents Form** (2nd edition)    TA10

**Address of the property**

Postcode ☐☐☐☐☐☐☐☐

**Full names of the seller**

**Seller's solicitor**
Name of solicitors firm

Address

Email

Reference number

**Definitions**

- 'Seller' means all sellers together where the property is owned by more than one person
- 'Buyer' means all buyers together where the property is being bought by more than one person

*SPECIMEN*

The Law Society    www.lawsociety.org.uk

© Law Society 2009. Reproduced with the assistance of Oyez Professional Services Limited.

# TA10 FITTINGS AND CONTENTS FORM

**Instructions to the seller and the buyer**

This form must be completed accurately by the seller. It may become part of the contract between the seller and the buyer.

The seller should make a clear statement of what is included in the sale of the property by marking each box in this form with a ✓ or a **X**, as shown below:

| Included in the sale of the property | ✓ |
|---|---|
| Not included in the sale of the property | X |

The seller may be prepared to sell to the buyer an item which is otherwise not included in the sale of the property. In this case, the seller should mark the appropriate box with a **X** to show the item is not included, followed by the amount that the seller wishes to be paid for the item, as shown below.

| Not included, but for sale at an extra cost | X{amount} |
|---|---|

The buyer can then decide whether to accept the seller's offer. The seller and buyer should inform their solicitors of any arrangements made about items offered for sale in this way.

If the seller removes any fixtures and fittings, the seller must make good any damage caused by their removal.

If the seller removes a light fitting, it is assumed that the seller will replace the fitting with a ceiling rose and socket, a flex, bulb holder and bulb.

The seller is responsible for removing any possessions, including rubbish, from the property, the garage, the garden and any outbuildings or sheds.

The seller and the buyer should check the information given on the form carefully.

APPENDIX B(IV)

## 1 Basic fittings

| | | | |
|---|---|---|---|
| Boiler / immersion heater | | Roof insulation | |
| Radiators / wall heaters | | Window fitments | |
| Night-storage heaters | | Window shutters / grills | |
| Free-standing heaters | | Internal door furniture | |
| Gas fires (with surround) | | External door furniture | |
| Electric fires (with surround) | | Doorbell / chime | |
| Light switches | | Electric sockets | |

## 2 Television and telephone

| | | | |
|---|---|---|---|
| Telephone receivers | | Television aerial | |
| Radio aerial | | Satellite dish | |

## 3 Kitchen

| | | | |
|---|---|---|---|
| Hob | | Refrigerator / fridge-freezer | |
| Extractor hood | | Freezer | |
| Fitted oven and grills | | Free-standing oven / cooker | |
| Fitted microwave | | Dishwasher | |
| Tumble-dryer | | Washing machine | |

## 4 Bathroom

| | | | |
|---|---|---|---|
| Bath | | Separate shower and fittings | |
| Shower fitting for bath | | Towel rail | |
| Shower curtain | | Soap / toothbrush holders | |
| Bathroom cabinet | | Toilet roll holders | |
| Taps | | Bathroom mirror | |

© Law Society 2009     3 of 4     Fittings and Contents Form TA10

TA10 FITTINGS AND CONTENTS FORM

### 5 Carpets, curtains, light fittings and fitted units

|  | Carpets | Curtain rails poles/pelmets* | Curtains/ blinds* | Light fittings | Fitted units** |
|---|---|---|---|---|---|
| Hall, stairs and landing | | | | | |
| Living room | | | | | |
| Dining room | | | | | |
| Kitchen | | | | | |
| Bedroom 1 | | | | | |
| Bedroom 2 | | | | | |
| Bedroom 3 | | | | | |
| | | | | | |
| | | | | | |
| | | | | | |

If the seller wishes to further explain the answers to section 5 above, please give details:

* Delete as appropriate.
** Fitted units (for example: fitted cupboards, fitted shelves, and fitted wardrobes).

### 6 Outdoor area

| Garden furniture | | Outdoor heater | |
|---|---|---|---|
| Garden ornaments | | Stock of fuel | |
| Trees, plants, shrubs | | Outside lights | |
| Barbecue | | Water butt | |
| Dustbins | | Clothes line | |
| Garden shed | | Rotary line | |
| Greenhouse | | | |

Signed: ........................................................................    Dated: ........................

Each seller should sign this form.

# APPENDIX B(V)

# TA13 Completion information and undertakings (2nd Edition)

## Completion information and undertakings (2nd edition)

**WARNING:** Replies to Requisitions 3.2 and 5.2 are treated as a solicitor's undertaking.

**Address of the property**

Postcode

**Seller**

**Buyer**

### 1 Vacant possession

**1.1** If vacant possession (of whole or part) is to be given on completion what arrangements will be made to hand over the keys?

- [ ] will be left with agents
- [ ] will be left with seller's solicitors
- [ ] other (please give details)

**1.2** If vacant possession (of whole or part) is not being given, please confirm that an authority to the tenant to pay the rent to the buyer will be handed over or be included with the documents to be remitted to the buyer's solicitors on completion.

- [ ] Confirmed

The Law Society

Page 1 of 4

TA13
© Law Society 2011
TA13/1

© Law Society 2011. Reproduced with the assistance of Oyez Professional Services Limited.

# TA13 COMPLETION INFORMATION AND UNDERTAKINGS

## 2 Deeds and documents

**2.1** If the title is unregistered, do you hold all of the title deeds?  ☐ Yes  ☐ No

If No, please give details:

**2.2** Please supply a list of the deeds and documents to be handed over or remitted to the buyer's solicitors on completion.  ☐ Enclosed

## 3 Completion

**3.1** Will completion take place at your office?  ☐ Yes  ☐ No

If No, where or how will it take place?

**WARNING: A reply to requisition 3.2 is treated as an undertaking. Great care must be taken when answering this requisition.**

**3.2** If we wish to complete through the post, please confirm that:

(a) You undertake to adopt the Law Society's Code for Completion by Post; and  ☐ Confirmed

(b) The mortgages and charges listed in reply to 5.1 are those specified for the purpose of paragraph 6 of the Code.  ☐ Confirmed

APPENDIX B(V)

### 4 Money

**4.1** Please state the exact amount payable on completion.

£ _____

☐ Enclosed  ☐ Not applicable

If it is not just the balance purchase money, please provide copy receipts for any rent or service charge or other payments being apportioned.

**4.2** Please provide details of your bank and the account to which completion monies are to be sent:

Name of bank

Address of bank

Branch sort code
☐☐ ☐☐ ☐☐

Client account name

Client account number

### 5 Mortgages and charges

**5.1** Please list the mortgages or charges secured on the property which you undertake to redeem or discharge to the extent that they relate to the property on or before completion (this includes repayment of any discount under the Housing Acts).

Page 3 of 4

Completion information and undertakings **TA13**
TA13/3

82

# TA13 COMPLETION INFORMATION AND UNDERTAKINGS

**WARNING: A reply to requisition 5.2 is treated as an undertaking. Great care must be taken when answering this requisition.**

5.2 Do you undertake to redeem or discharge the mortgages and charges listed in reply to 5.1 on completion and to send to us Form DS1, DS3, the receipted charge(s) or confirmation that notice of release or discharge in electronic form has been given to the Land Registry as soon as you receive them?

☐ Yes   ☐ No

5.3 If you **DO NOT** agree to adopt the current Law Society's Code for Completion by Post, please confirm that you are the duly authorised agent of the proprietor of every mortgage or charge on the property which you have undertaken, in reply to 5.2, to redeem or discharge.

☐ Confirmed

**WARNING: These replies should be signed only by a person with authority to give undertakings on behalf of the firm.**

Buyer's solicitor

Date ☐☐/☐☐/☐☐

Seller's solicitor

Date ☐☐/☐☐/☐☐

APPENDIX C

# Standard Conditions of Sale (fifth edition) (including Explanatory Notes)[1]

CONVEYANCER'S RECORD OF EXCHANGE

Name of buyer's conveyancer:

Name of seller's conveyancer:

Law Society formula  A / B / C / Personal Exchange

THE INFORMATION ABOVE DOES NOT FORM PART OF THE CONTRACT

**CONTRACT**
**INCORPORATING THE STANDARD CONDITIONS OF SALE**
**(FIFTH EDITION)**

| | |
|---|---|
| **Date** | : |
| **Seller** | : |
| **Buyer** | : |
| **Property (freehold/leasehold)** | : |
| **Title number/root of title** | : |
| **Specified incumbrances** | : |
| **Title guarantee (full/limited)** | : |
| **Completion date** | : |
| **Contract rate** | : |
| **Purchase price** | : |
| **Deposit** | : |
| **Contents price (if separate)** | : |
| **Balance** | : |

The seller will sell and the buyer will buy the property for the purchase price.

| WARNING | Signed |
|---|---|

---

[1] © Oyez (The Solicitors' Law Stationery Society Ltd) and the Law Society 2011.

STANDARD CONDITIONS OF SALE (FIFTH EDITION)

> This is a formal document, designed to create legal rights and legal obligations. Take advice before using it.
>
> Seller/Buyer

# STANDARD CONDITIONS OF SALE (FIFTH EDITION)
# (NATIONAL CONDITIONS OF SALE 25TH EDITION, LAW SOCIETY'S CONDITIONS OF SALE 2011)

## 1. GENERAL

### 1.1 Definitions

1.1.1 In these conditions:
    (a) 'accrued interest' means:

        (i) if money has been placed on deposit or in a building society share account, the interest actually earned
        (ii) otherwise, the interest which might reasonably have been earned by depositing the money at interest on seven days' notice of withdrawal with a clearing bank less, in either case, any proper charges for handling the money

    (b) 'clearing bank' means a bank which is a shareholder in CHAPS Clearing Co. Limited
    (c) 'completion date' has the meaning given in condition 6.1.1
    (d) 'contents price' means any separate amount payable for contents included in the contract
    (e) 'contract rate' means the Law Society's interest rate from time to time in force
    (f) 'conveyancer' means a solicitor, barrister, duly certified notary public, licensed conveyancer or recognised body under sections 9 or 23 of the Administration of Justice Act 1985
    (g) 'lease' includes sub-lease, tenancy and agreement for a lease or sub-lease
    (h) 'mortgage' means a mortgage or charge securing the repayment of money
    (i) 'notice to complete' means a notice requiring completion of the contract in accordance with condition 6.8
    (j) 'public requirement' means any notice, order or proposal given or made (whether before or after the date of the contract) by a body acting on statutory authority
    (k) 'requisition' includes objection
    (l) 'transfer' includes conveyance and assignment
    (m) 'working day' means any day from Monday to Friday (inclusive) which is not Christmas Day, Good Friday or a statutory Bank Holiday.

1.1.2 In these conditions the terms 'absolute title' and 'official copies' have the special meanings given to them by the Land Registration Act 2002.

1.1.3 A party is ready, able and willing to complete:
    (a) if he could be, but for the default of the other party, and

APPENDIX C

        (b)    in the case of the seller, even though the property remains subject to a mortgage, if the amount to be paid on completion enables the property to be transferred freed of all mortgages (except any to which the sale is expressly subject).

1.1.4    These conditions apply except as varied or excluded by the contract.

**1.2    Joint parties**

If there is more than one seller or more than one buyer, the obligations which they undertake can be enforced against them all jointly or against each individually.

**1.3    Notices and documents**

1.3.1    A notice required or authorised by the contract must be in writing.

1.3.2    Giving a notice or delivering a document to a party's conveyancer has the same effect as giving or delivering it to that party.

1.3.3    Where delivery of the original document is not essential, a notice or document is validly given or sent if it is sent:
        (a)    by fax, or
        (b)    by e-mail to an e-mail address for the intended recipient given in the contract.

1.3.4    Subject to conditions 1.3.5 to 1.3.7, a notice is given and a document is delivered when it is received.
1.3.5    (a)    A notice or document sent through a document exchange is received when it is available for collection.
        (b)    A notice or document which is received after 4.00 pm on a working day, or on a day which is not a working day, is to be treated as having been received on the next working day.
        (c)    An automated response to a notice or document sent by e-mail that the intended recipient is out of the office is to be treated as proof that the notice or document was not received.

1.3.6    Condition 1.3.7 applies unless there is proof:
        (a)    that a notice or document has not been received, or
        (b)    of when it was received.

1.3.7    A notice or document sent by the following means is treated as having been received as follows:
        (a)    by first-class post: before 4.00 pm on the second working day after posting
        (b)    by second-class post: before 4.00 pm on the third working day after posting
        (c)    through a document exchange: before 4.00 pm on the first working day after the day on which it would normally be available for collection by the addressee
        (d)    by fax: one hour after despatch
        (e)    by e-mail: before 4.00 pm on the first working day after despatch.

**1.4    VAT**

1.4.1    The purchase price and the contents price are inclusive of any value added tax.

1.4.2 All other sums made payable by the contract are exclusive of any value added tax and where a supply is made which is chargeable to value added tax, the recipient of the supply is to pay the supplier (in addition to any other amounts payable under the contract) a sum equal to the value added tax chargeable on that supply.

## 1.5 Assignment and sub-sales

1.5.1 The buyer is not entitled to transfer the benefit of the contract.

1.5.2 The seller cannot be required to transfer the property in parts or to any person other than the buyer.

## 1.6 Third party rights

Unless otherwise expressly stated nothing in this contract will create rights pursuant to the Contracts (Rights of Third Parties) Act 1999 in favour of anyone other than the parties to the contract.

# 2. FORMATION

## 2.1 Date

2.1.1 If the parties intend to make a contract by exchanging duplicate copies by post or through a document exchange, the contract is made when the last copy is posted or deposited at the document exchange.

2.1.2 If the parties' conveyancers agree to treat exchange as taking place before duplicate copies are actually exchanged, the contract is made as so agreed.

## 2.2 Deposit

2.2.1 The buyer is to pay or send a deposit of 10 per cent of the purchase price no later than the date of the contract.

2.2.2 If a cheque tendered in payment of all or part of the deposit is dishonoured when first presented, the seller may, within seven working days of being notified that the cheque has been dishonoured, give notice to the buyer that the contract is discharged by the buyer's breach.

2.2.3 Conditions 2.2.4 to 2.2.6 do not apply on a sale by auction.

2.2.4 The deposit is to be paid:
 (a) by electronic means from an account held in the name of a conveyancer at a clearing bank to an account in the name of the seller's conveyancer or (in a case where condition 2.2.5 applies) a conveyancer nominated by him and maintained at a clearing bank, or
 (b) to the seller's conveyancer or (in a case where condition 2.2.5 applies) a conveyancer nominated by him by cheque drawn on a solicitor's or licensed conveyancer's client account.

2.2.5 If before completion date the seller agrees to buy another property in England and Wales for his residence, he may use all or any part of the deposit as a deposit in that transaction to be held on terms to the same effect as this condition and condition 2.2.6.

APPENDIX C

2.2.6 Any deposit or part of a deposit not being used in accordance with condition 2.2.5 is to be held by the seller's conveyancer as stakeholder on terms that on completion it is paid to the seller with accrued interest.

**2.3 Auctions**

2.3.1 On a sale by auction the following conditions apply to the property and, if it is sold in lots, to each lot.

2.3.2 The sale is subject to a reserve price.

2.3.3 The seller, or a person on his behalf, may bid up to the reserve price.

2.3.4 The auctioneer may refuse any bid.

2.3.5 If there is a dispute about a bid, the auctioneer may resolve the dispute or restart the auction at the last undisputed bid.

2.3.6 The deposit is to be paid to the auctioneer as agent for the seller.

**3. MATTERS AFFECTING THE PROPERTY**

**3.1 Freedom from incumbrances**

3.1.1 The seller is selling the property free from incumbrances, other than those mentioned in condition 3.1.2.

3.1.2 The incumbrances subject to which the property is sold are:
  (a) those specified in the contract
  (b) those discoverable by inspection of the property before the date of the contract
  (c) those the seller does not and could not reasonably know about
  (d) those, other than mortgages, which the buyer knows about
  (e) entries made before the date of the contract in any public register except those maintained by the Land Registry or its Land Charges Department or by Companies House
  (f) public requirements.

3.1.3 After the contract is made, the seller is to give the buyer written details without delay of any new public requirement and of anything in writing which he learns about concerning a matter covered by condition 3.1.2.

3.1.4 The buyer is to bear the cost of complying with any outstanding public requirement and is to indemnify the seller against any liability resulting from a public requirement.

**3.2 Physical state**

3.2.1 The buyer accepts the property in the physical state it is in at the date of the contract unless the seller is building or converting it.

3.2.2 A leasehold property is sold subject to any subsisting breach of a condition or tenant's obligation relating to the physical state of the property which renders the lease liable to forfeiture.

3.2.3　A sub-lease is granted subject to any subsisting breach of a condition or tenant's obligation relating to the physical state of the property which renders the seller's own lease liable to forfeiture.

## 3.3　Leases affecting the property

3.3.1　The following provisions apply if any part of the property is sold subject to a lease.

3.3.2
- (a) The seller having provided the buyer with full details of each lease or copies of the documents embodying the lease terms, the buyer is treated as entering into the contract knowing and fully accepting those terms.
- (b) The seller is to inform the buyer without delay if the lease ends or if the seller learns of any application by the tenant in connection with the lease; the seller is then to act as the buyer reasonably directs, and the buyer is to indemnify him against all consequent loss and expense.
- (c) Except with the buyer's consent, the seller is not to agree to any proposal to change the lease terms nor to take any step to end the lease.
- (d) The seller is to inform the buyer without delay of any change to the lease terms which may be proposed or agreed.
- (e) The buyer is to indemnify the seller against all claims arising from the lease after actual completion; this includes claims which are unenforceable against a buyer for want of registration.
- (f) The seller takes no responsibility for what rent is lawfully recoverable, nor for whether or how any legislation affects the lease.
- (g) If the let land is not wholly within the property, the seller may apportion the rent.

## 4.　TITLE AND TRANSFER

### 4.1　Proof of title

4.1.1　Without cost to the buyer, the seller is to provide the buyer with proof of the title to the property and of his ability to transfer it, or to procure its transfer.

4.1.2　Where the property has a registered title the proof is to include official copies of the items referred to in rules 134(1)(a) and (b) and 135(1)(a) of the Land Registration Rules 2003, so far as they are not to be discharged or overridden at or before completion.

4.1.3　Where the property has an unregistered title, the proof is to include:
- (a) an abstract of title or an epitome of title with photocopies of the documents, and
- (b) production of every document or an abstract, epitome or copy of it with an original marking by a conveyancer either against the original or an examined abstract or an examined copy.

### 4.2　Requisitions

4.2.1　The buyer may not raise requisitions:
- (a) on any title shown by the seller before the contract was made
- (b) in relation to the matters covered by condition 3.1.2.

4.2.2　Notwithstanding condition 4.2.1, the buyer may, within six working days of a matter coming to his attention after the contract was made, raise written requisitions on that matter. In that event, steps 3 and 4 in condition 4.3.1 apply.

APPENDIX C

4.2.3 On the expiry of the relevant time limit under condition 4.2.2 or condition 4.3.1, the buyer loses his right to raise requisitions or to make observations.

**4.3 Timetable**

4.3.1 Subject to condition 4.2 and to the extent that the seller did not take the steps described in condition 4.1.1 before the contract was made, the following are the steps for deducing and investigating the title to the property to be taken within the following time limits:

| Step | Time Limit |
| --- | --- |
| 1. The seller is to comply with condition 4.1.1 | Immediately after making the contract |
| 2. The buyer may raise written requisitions | Six working days after either the date of the contract or the date of delivery of the seller's evidence of title on which the requisitions are raised whichever is the later |
| 3. The seller is to reply in writing to any requisitions raised | Four working days after receiving the requisitions |
| 4. The buyer may make written observations on the seller's replies | Three working days after receiving the replies |

The time limit on the buyer's right to raise requisitions applies even where the seller supplies incomplete evidence of his title, but the buyer may, within six working days from delivery of any further evidence, raise further requisitions resulting from that evidence.

4.3.2 The parties are to take the following steps to prepare and agree the transfer of the property within the following time limits:

| Step | Time Limit |
| --- | --- |
| A. The buyer is to send the seller a draft transfer | At least twelve working days before completion date |
| B. The seller is to approve or revise that draft and either return it or retain it for use as the actual transfer | Four working days after delivery of the draft transfer |
| C. If the draft is returned the buyer is to send an engrossment to the seller | At least five working days before completion date |

4.3.3 Periods of time under conditions 4.3.1 and 4.3.2 may run concurrently.

4.3.4 If the period between the date of the contract and completion date is less than 15 working days, the time limits in conditions 4.2.2, 4.3.1 and 4.3.2 are to be reduced by the same proportion as that period bears to the period of 15 working days. Fractions of a working day are to be rounded down except that the time limit to perform any step is not to be less than one working day.

**4.4 Defining the property**

The seller need not:

STANDARD CONDITIONS OF SALE (FIFTH EDITION)

(a) prove the exact boundaries of the property
(b) prove who owns fences, ditches, hedges or walls
(c) separately identify parts of the property with different titles further than he may be able to do from information in his possession.

## 4.5 Rents and rentcharges

The fact that a rent or rentcharge, whether payable or receivable by the owner of the property, has been, or will on completion be, informally apportioned is not to be regarded as a defect in title.

## 4.6 Transfer

4.6.1 The buyer does not prejudice his right to raise requisitions, or to require replies to any raised, by taking any steps in relation to preparing or agreeing the transfer.

4.6.2 Subject to condition 4.6.3, the seller is to transfer the property with full title guarantee.

4.6.3 The transfer is to have effect as if the disposition is expressly made subject to all matters covered by condition 3.1.2 and, if the property is leasehold, is to contain a statement that the covenants set out in section 4 of the Law of Property (Miscellaneous Provisions) Act 1994 will not extend to any breach of the tenant's covenants in the lease relating to the physical state of the property.

4.6.4 If after completion the seller will remain bound by any obligation affecting the property which was disclosed to the buyer before the contract was made, but the law does not imply any covenant by the buyer to indemnify the seller against liability for future breaches of it:
(a) the buyer is to covenant in the transfer to indemnify the seller against liability for any future breach of the obligation and to perform it from then on, and
(b) if required by the seller, the buyer is to execute and deliver to the seller on completion a duplicate transfer prepared by the buyer.

4.6.5 The seller is to arrange at his expense that, in relation to every document of title which the buyer does not receive on completion, the buyer is to have the benefit of:
(a) a written acknowledgement of his right to its production, and
(b) a written undertaking for its safe custody (except while it is held by a mortgagee or by someone in a fiduciary capacity).

## 4.7 Membership of company

Where the seller is, or is required to be, a member of a company that has an interest in the property or has management responsibilities for the property or the surrounding areas, the seller is, without cost to the buyer, to provide such documents on completion as will enable the buyer to become a member of that company.

## 5. RISK, INSURANCE AND OCCUPATION PENDING COMPLETION

5.1.1 The property is at the risk of the buyer from the date of the contract.

5.1.2 The seller is under no obligation to the buyer to insure the property unless:

APPENDIX C

        (a)    the contract provides that a policy effected by or for the seller and insuring the property or any part of it against liability for loss or damage is to continue in force, or

        (b)    the property or any part of it is let on terms under which the seller (whether as landlord or as tenant) is obliged to insure against loss or damage.

5.1.3    If the seller is obliged to insure the property under condition 5.1.2, the seller is to:
        (a)    do everything necessary to maintain the policy
        (b)    permit the buyer to inspect the policy or evidence of its terms
        (c)    if before completion the property suffers loss or damage:
                (i)    pay to the buyer on completion the amount of the policy monies which the seller has received, so far as not applied in repairing or reinstating the property, and
                (ii)   if no final payment has then been received, assign to the buyer, at the buyer's expense, all rights to claim under the policy in such form as the buyer reasonably requires and pending execution of the assignment hold any policy monies received in trust for the buyer
        (d)    cancel the policy on completion.

5.1.4    Where the property is leasehold and the property, or any building containing it, is insured by a reversioner or other third party, the seller is to use reasonable efforts to ensure that the insurance is maintained until completion and if, before completion, the property or building suffers loss or damage the seller is to assign to the buyer on completion, at the buyer's expense, such rights as the seller may have in the policy monies, in such form as the buyer reasonably requires.

5.1.5    If payment under a policy effected by or for the buyer is reduced, because the property is covered against loss or damage by an insurance policy effected by or on behalf of the seller, then, unless the seller is obliged to insure the property under condition 5.1.2, the purchase price is to be abated by the amount of that reduction.

5.1.6    Section 47 of the Law of Property Act 1925 does not apply.

### 5.2    Occupation by buyer

5.2.1    If the buyer is not already lawfully in the property, and the seller agrees to let him into occupation, the buyer occupies on the following terms.

5.2.2    The buyer is a licensee and not a tenant. The terms of the licence are that the buyer:
        (a)    cannot transfer it
        (b)    may permit members of his household to occupy the property
        (c)    is to pay or indemnify the seller against all outgoings and other expenses in respect of the property
        (d)    is to pay the seller a fee calculated at the contract rate on a sum equal to the purchase price (less any deposit paid) for the period of the licence
        (e)    is entitled to any rents and profits from any part of the property which he does not occupy
        (f)    is to keep the property in as good a state of repair as it was in when he went into occupation (except for fair wear and tear) and is not to alter it
        (g)    if the property is leasehold, is not to do anything which puts the seller in breach of his obligations in the lease, and
        (h)    is to quit the property when the licence ends.

5.2.3  The buyer is not in occupation for the purposes of this condition if he merely exercises rights of access given solely to do work agreed by the seller.

5.2.4  The buyer's licence ends on the earliest of: completion date, rescission of the contract or when five working days' notice given by one party to the other takes effect.

5.2.5  If the buyer is in occupation of the property after his licence has come to an end and the contract is subsequently completed he is to pay the seller compensation for his continued occupation calculated at the same rate as the fee mentioned in condition 5.2.2(d).

5.2.6  The buyer's right to raise requisitions is unaffected.

## 6. COMPLETION

### 6.1 Date

6.1.1  Completion date is twenty working days after the date of the contract but time is not of the essence of the contract unless a notice to complete has been served.

6.1.2  If the money due on completion is received after 2.00 pm, completion is to be treated, for the purposes only of conditions 6.3 and 7.2, as taking place on the next working day as a result of the buyer's default.

6.1.3  Condition 6.1.2 does not apply and the seller is treated as in default if:
    (a)  the sale is with vacant possession of the property or any part of it, and
    (b)  the buyer is ready, able and willing to complete but does not pay the money due on completion until after 2.00 pm because the seller has not vacated the property or that part by that time.

### 6.2 Arrangements and place

6.2.1  The buyer's conveyancer and the seller's conveyancer are to co-operate in agreeing arrangements for completing the contract.

6.2.2  Completion is to take place in England and Wales, either at the seller's conveyancer's office or at some other place which the seller reasonably specifies.

### 6.3 Apportionments

6.3.1  On evidence of proper payment being made, income and outgoings of the property are to be apportioned between the parties so far as the change of ownership on completion will affect entitlement to receive or liability to pay them.

6.3.2  If the whole property is sold with vacant possession or the seller exercises his option in condition 7.2.4, apportionment is to be made with effect from the date of actual completion; otherwise, it is to be made from completion date.

6.3.3  In apportioning any sum, it is to be assumed that the seller owns the property until the end of the day from which apportionment is made and that the sum accrues from day to day at the rate at which it is payable on that day.

6.3.4  For the purpose of apportioning income and outgoings, it is to be assumed that they accrue at an equal daily rate throughout the year.

APPENDIX C

6.3.5 When a sum to be apportioned is not known or easily ascertainable at completion, a provisional apportionment is to be made according to the best estimate available. As soon as the amount is known, a final apportionment is to be made and notified to the other party. Any resulting balance is to be paid no more than ten working days later, and if not then paid the balance is to bear interest at the contract rate from then until payment.

6.3.6 Compensation payable under condition 5.2.5 is not to be apportioned.

### 6.4 Amount payable

The amount payable by the buyer on completion is the purchase price and the contents price (less any deposit already paid to the seller or his agent) adjusted to take account of:
- (a) apportionments made under condition 6.3
- (b) any compensation to be paid or allowed under condition 7.2.

### 6.5 Title deeds

6.5.1 As soon as the buyer has complied with all his obligations under this contract on completion the seller must hand over the documents of title.

6.5.2 Condition 6.5.1 does not apply to any documents of title relating to land being retained by the seller after completion.

### 6.6 Rent receipts

The buyer is to assume that whoever gave any receipt for a payment of rent or service charge which the seller produces was the person or the agent of the person then entitled to that rent or service charge.

### 6.7 Means of payment

The buyer is to pay the money due on completion by a direct transfer of cleared funds from an account held in the name of a conveyancer at a clearing bank and, if appropriate, an unconditional release of a deposit held by a stakeholder.

### 6.8 Notice to complete

6.8.1 At any time after the time applicable under condition 6.1.2 on completion date, a party who is ready, able and willing to complete may give the other a notice to complete.

6.8.2 The parties are to complete the contract within ten working days of giving a notice to complete, excluding the day on which the notice is given. For this purpose, time is of the essence of the contract.

6.8.3 On receipt of a notice to complete:
- (a) if the buyer paid no deposit, he is forthwith to pay a deposit of 10 per cent
- (b) if the buyer paid a deposit of less than 10 per cent, he is forthwith to pay a further deposit equal to the balance of that 10 per cent.

## 7. REMEDIES

### 7.1 Errors and omissions

7.1.1 If any plan or statement in the contract, or in the negotiations leading to it, is or was misleading or inaccurate due to an error or omission by the seller, the remedies available to the buyer are as follows.
    (a) When there is a material difference between the description or value of the property, or of any of the contents included in the contract, as represented and as it is, the buyer is entitled to damages.
    (b) An error or omission only entitles the buyer to rescind the contract:
        (i) where it results from fraud or recklessness, or
        (ii) where he would be obliged, to his prejudice, to accept property differing substantially (in quantity, quality or tenure) from what the error or omission had led him to expect.

7.1.2 If either party rescinds the contract:
    (a) unless the rescission is a result of the buyer's breach of contract the deposit is to be repaid to the buyer with accrued interest
    (b) the buyer is to return any documents he received from the seller and is to cancel any registration of the contract.

### 7.2 Late completion

7.2.1 If there is default by either or both of the parties in performing their obligations under the contract and completion is delayed, the party whose total period of default is the greater is to pay compensation to the other party.

7.2.2 Compensation is calculated at the contract rate on an amount equal to the purchase price, less (where the buyer is the paying party) any deposit paid, for the period by which the paying party's default exceeds that of the receiving party, or, if shorter, the period between completion date and actual completion.

7.2.3 Any claim for loss resulting from delayed completion is to be reduced by any compensation paid under this contract.

7.2.4 Where the buyer holds the property as tenant of the seller and completion is delayed, the seller may give notice to the buyer, before the date of actual completion, that he intends to take the net income from the property until completion. If he does so, he cannot claim compensation under condition 7.2.1 as well.

### 7.3 After completion

Completion does not cancel liability to perform any outstanding obligation under this contract.

### 7.4 Buyer's failure to comply with notice to complete

7.4.1 If the buyer fails to complete in accordance with a notice to complete, the following terms apply.

7.4.2 The seller may rescind the contract, and if he does so:

APPENDIX C

    (a) he may:
        (i) forfeit and keep any deposit and accrued interest
        (ii) resell the property and any contents included in the contract
        (iii) claim damages
    (b) the buyer is to return any documents he received from the seller and is to cancel any registration of the contract.

7.4.3 The seller retains his other rights and remedies.

### 7.5 Seller's failure to comply with notice to complete

7.5.1 If the seller fails to complete in accordance with a notice to complete, the following terms apply.

7.5.2 The buyer may rescind the contract, and if he does so:
    (a) the deposit is to be repaid to the buyer with accrued interest
    (b) the buyer is to return any documents he received from the seller and is, at the seller's expense, to cancel any registration of the contract.

7.5.3 The buyer retains his other rights and remedies.

## 8. LEASEHOLD PROPERTY

### 8.1 Existing leases

8.1.1 The following provisions apply to a sale of leasehold land.

8.1.2 The seller having provided the buyer with copies of the documents embodying the lease terms, the buyer is treated as entering into the contract knowing and fully accepting those terms.

### 8.2 New leases

8.2.1 The following provisions apply to a contract to grant a new lease.

8.2.2 The conditions apply so that:

    'seller' means the proposed landlord

    'buyer' means the proposed tenant

    'purchase price' means the premium to be paid on the grant of a lease.

8.2.3 The lease is to be in the form of the draft attached to the contract.

8.2.4 If the term of the new lease will exceed seven years, the seller is to deduce a title which will enable the buyer to register the lease at the Land Registry with an absolute title.

8.2.5 The seller is to engross the lease and a counterpart of it and is to send the counterpart to the buyer at least five working days before completion date.

8.2.6 The buyer is to execute the counterpart and deliver it to the seller on completion.

## 8.3 Consent

8.3.1   (a)   The following provisions apply if a consent to let, assign or sub-let is required to complete the contract.

(b)   In this condition 'consent' means consent in the form which satisfies the requirement to obtain it.

8.3.2   (a)   The seller is to apply for the consent at his expense, and to use all reasonable efforts to obtain it.

(b)   The buyer is to provide all information and references reasonably required.

8.3.3 Unless he is in breach of his obligation under condition 8.3.2, either party may rescind the contract by notice to the other party if three working days before completion date (or before a later date on which the parties have agreed to complete the contract):

  (a)   the consent has not been given, or

  (b)   the consent has been given subject to a condition to which a party reasonably objects. In that case, neither party is to be treated as in breach of contract and condition 7.1.2 applies.

## 9. CONTENTS

9.1 The following provisions apply to any contents which are included in the contract, whether or not a separate price is to be paid for them.

9.2 The contract takes effect as a contract for sale of goods.

9.3 The buyer takes the contents in the physical state they are in at the date of the contract.

9.4 Ownership of the contents passes to the buyer on actual completion.

## SPECIAL CONDITIONS

1   (a)   This contract incorporates the Standard Conditions of Sale (Fifth Edition).

  (b)   The terms used in this contract have the same meaning when used in the Conditions.

2 Subject to the terms of this contract and to the Standard Conditions of Sale, the seller is to transfer the property with either full title guarantee or limited title guarantee, as specified on the front page.

3   (a)   The sale includes those contents which are indicated on the attached list as included in the sale and the buyer is to pay the contents price for them.

  (b)   The sale excludes those fixtures which are at the property and are indicated on the attached list as excluded from the sale.

4 The property is sold with vacant possession.

(or)

4 The property is sold subject to the following leases or tenancies:

5 Conditions 6.1.2 and 6.1.3 shall take effect as if the time specified in them were [_____] rather than 2.00 pm.

APPENDIX C

## 6 Representations

Neither party can rely on any representation made by the other, unless made in writing by the other or his conveyancer, but this does not exclude liability for fraud or recklessness.

## 7 Occupier's consent

Each occupier identified below agrees with the seller and the buyer, in consideration of their entering into this contract, that the occupier concurs in the sale of the property on the terms of this contract, undertakes to vacate the property on or before the completion date and releases the property and any included fixtures and contents from any right or interest that the occupier may have.

**Note:** this condition does not apply to occupiers under leases or tenancies subject to which the property is sold

Name(s) and signature(s) of the occupier(s) (if any):

Name……………………………………………

Signature………………………………………..

Notices may be sent to:

**Seller's conveyancer's name:**
  E-mail address:*

**Buyer's conveyancer's name:**
  E-mail address:*

*Adding an e-mail address authorises service by e-mail: see condition 1.3.3(b).


# EXPLANATORY NOTES ON THE STANDARD CONDITIONS OF SALE (FIFTH EDITION) (APRIL 2011)

## GENERAL

The fifth edition of the Standard Conditions of Sale (the 'SCS') takes effect on 1 April 2011 and supersedes the fourth edition of the SCS issued in October 2003.

The revisions to the fourth edition have been made to bring the SCS in line with current law and practice with the aim of reducing the need for special conditions. The changes are intended to achieve a balance between the interests of the buyer and seller.

The main change is that, reflecting the position under the general law, the buyer is now to assume the risk from the date of exchange. Nonetheless, as explained below, there are certain cases in which the seller is obliged to insure.

The SCS are intended primarily for use in residential sales. Although they may be suitable for the sale of small business premises, conveyancers are likely to find that, for most commercial transactions, the Standard Commercial Property Conditions (the 'SCPC') are better suited to their needs.

The revisions maintain the policy of using plain English rather than legal terminology where possible.

The fifth edition of the SCS represents the 25th edition of the National Conditions of Sale and the Law Society's Conditions of Sale 2011.

## DEFINITIONS

### 'contents price'

Condition 1.1.1(d) now refers to 'contents' rather than 'chattels'.

### 'direct credit'

The previous definition of 'direct credit' (meaning a 'direct transfer of cleared funds to an account nominated by the seller's conveyancer and maintained by a clearing bank') has been deleted, since this concept is now used only in condition 6.7. See also the explanation of the changes to condition 2.2.4.

### 'mortgage'

A new definition of 'mortgage' has been added, which clarifies the meaning of the term in condition 1.1.3(b) and is used in the new paragraph (d) of condition 3.1.2.

## VAT

Condition 1.4.1 has been amended to make it clear that the agreed purchase price and contents price for a property are inclusive of VAT. This reflects the fact that the SCS are intended primarily to be used for residential transactions, which are usually exempt for VAT purposes.

If the sale does constitute a chargeable supply for VAT purposes, a special condition should be inserted if the seller requires the buyer to pay a sum equal to the VAT. In commercial or mixed use transactions, it is likely to be more appropriate to use the SCPC.

By virtue of condition 1.4.2, any other sums payable under the contract (i.e. sums other than the purchase price and contents price) will continue to be exclusive of VAT. In these circumstances, the recipient of a taxable supply will be liable to pay to the supplier a sum equal to the VAT chargeable on that supply.

## ASSIGNMENT AND SUB-SALES

A new condition 1.5.2 provides that the seller cannot be required to transfer the property, or any part of it, to any person other than the buyer. The amendment is intended to protect the seller from becoming involved in a transaction with an unknown third party. This change clarifies the position and ensures consistency with the SCPC.

## THIRD PARTY RIGHTS

Condition 1.6 has been added to exclude the operation of the Contracts (Rights of Third Parties) Act 1999. This ensures that a third party will not have any rights under the contract by virtue of that Act.

APPENDIX C

## DEPOSIT

Condition 2.2.1 has been amended so that the 10% deposit is calculated by reference only to the purchase price and not, as before, the total of the purchase price and any separate contents price. This has been changed in order to provide certainty at an early stage as to the amount of the deposit that will be required. The buyer will not be required to pay 10% of the contents price, which can still be the subject of negotiation up until the point at which contracts are exchanged. If the deposit is also to take account of the contents price, this should be provided for by special condition. This change largely reflects practice.

As noted above, the definition of 'direct credit' has been deleted from the SCS. In condition 2.2.4, reference to 'direct credit' has been replaced by a reference to the deposit being paid by 'electronic means'. This has the effect that, unlike payments due on completion, the deposit does not have to be paid in cleared funds. Additional wording has been inserted so that the money transfer must now be made from an account held in the name of a conveyancer at a clearing bank to an account maintained at a clearing bank held in the name of either the seller's conveyancer or, where condition 2.2.5 applies, a conveyancer higher up the chain. It is hoped that limiting payments to those from a conveyancer's account will assist the seller's conveyancer in complying with anti-money laundering obligations. Express provision by way of special condition will be required for any alternative arrangements. Condition 2.2.4(b) continues to make provision for the payment of the deposit by cheque but, where condition 2.2.5 applies, now permits the cheque to be made payable to a conveyancer higher up the chain.

## MATTERS AFFECTING THE PROPERTY

Condition 3.1.2(d) has been added to provide that the property is sold subject to any incumbrances (other than mortgages) which the buyer knows about. It is not considered fair for a buyer to be able to take action against a seller in respect of a matter which he knew about, but which was not expressly a matter subject to which the property was sold.

## RETAINED LAND

Condition 3.4 in the fourth edition of the SCS has been deleted. It sought to deal with the situation where land is retained by the seller. Issues relating to retained land, such as rights and covenants, should be dealt with by way of special condition and by annexing an agreed form of transfer.

## REQUISITIONS

The wording of condition 4.2.1(a) has been slightly amended to make it clear that the buyer cannot raise requisitions on any title shown by the seller before the contract was made. This is consistent with practice where title is deduced in full before exchange.

## DEFINING THE PROPERTY

Condition 4.4.2 of the fourth edition has been deleted so that the buyer can no longer require the seller to provide a statutory declaration about facts relevant to matters such as boundaries, hedges, ditches and walls. It is not considered to be reasonable to expect the seller to provide a statutory declaration after exchange of contracts when investigation of title has taken place prior to exchange.

If necessary, this issue should be dealt with by special condition.

## STANDARD CONDITIONS OF SALE (FIFTH EDITION)

## TRANSFER

The wording in condition 4.6.3 has been amended. In the case of a transfer of leasehold property, the contract requires the transfer to contain an express statement modifying the title guarantee by excluding the operation of section 4 of the Law of Property (Miscellaneous Provisions) Act 1994 in respect of any breach of the tenant's covenants in the lease relating to the physical state of the property. This has been inserted because similar provisions are widely used in practice and it is consistent with condition 3.2.2.

## MEMBERSHIP OF COMPANY

Condition 4.7 has been inserted to enable the buyer to become a member of a management company or any other relevant company that has an interest in the property. This addition will reduce the need for a special condition to deal with this point. The condition stipulates that all relevant documents (which may include membership or share certificates and/or a duly signed stock transfer form) are to be provided to the buyer on completion. The condition has been drafted to apply not only to those companies with responsibilities in relation to leasehold property but also to those which have management obligations in relation to freehold property.

## RISK, INSURANCE AND OCCUPATION PENDING COMPLETION

Significant changes have been made to the conditions relating to risk and insurance. The principal effect is that the risk position is reversed (from that in the fourth edition of the SCS) and the buyer bears the risk from exchange. Previous editions of the SCS left the risk with the seller until completion and, in practice, special conditions were frequently included to make the buyer bear the risk from exchange. This change brings the SCS broadly into line with the SCPC.

Even though the buyer takes the risk from exchange (meaning he still has to complete if the property is destroyed between exchange and completion), the seller may still have an obligation to insure the property between exchange and completion by virtue of condition 5.1.2. Under this condition, the seller is obliged to insure if the contract so provides or if the property is leasehold and the seller (whether as landlord or as tenant) is obliged to insure under the terms of the lease.

Condition 5.1.3 sets out the seller's obligations where he is required to insure.

Under condition 5.1.4, where the property is leasehold and insurance is effected by a landlord or other third party, the seller is to use reasonable efforts to ensure that the insurance is maintained until completion and if, before completion, the building suffers any loss or damage, the seller is to assign to the buyer any rights that the seller may have in the policy monies.

Condition 5.1.5 has been added in an attempt to clarify the position as regards 'double insurance'. This is where both the seller and buyer insure the property between exchange and completion. The new condition provides that where a payment under the buyer's insurance is reduced because the property is covered under an insurance policy taken out by or on behalf of the seller, then, provided the seller is not obliged to insure the property under condition 5.1.2, the purchase price is to be abated by the amount of that reduction. The position in this respect is now similar to that under the SCPC.

## OCCUPATION BY BUYER

Condition 5.2.2(d) has been amended in line with condition 2.2.1 so that the licence fee is to be calculated by reference to the purchase price only.

Condition 5.2.2(g) of the fourth edition of the SCS, which dealt with the buyer's duty to insure the property, has been deleted because the risk will have passed to the buyer under the amended condition 5.1. The new condition 5.2.2(g) stipulates that, if the property is leasehold, the buyer is not to do anything which puts the seller in breach of his obligations in the lease.

## APPORTIONMENTS

Condition 6.3.1 has been amended to require the party requesting apportionment to provide evidence of payment in relation to the relevant income and outgoings of the property.

## TITLE DEEDS

The wording in condition 6.5.1 has been slightly amended so that the reference to the buyer's obligations is expressly limited to those under the SCS.

## MEANS OF PAYMENT

The wording in condition 6.7 has been amended and now refers to a 'direct transfer' of cleared funds on completion. The previous edition used the defined term 'direct credit' which, as noted above, has been deleted in these conditions. This new wording makes it clear that the completion monies should come from and be paid to an account held in the name of a conveyancer. As with conditions 1.5.2 and 2.2.4, this change was made with the aim of combating fraud and assisting compliance with anti-money laundering measures.

## NOTICE TO COMPLETE

Condition 6.8.1 has been amended so that notice to complete cannot be given before 2 pm on the day of completion. This change is intended to prevent the seller from serving a notice to complete on the morning of completion date.

## LATE COMPLETION

Under condition 7.2.2, and in line with other relevant provisions in the SCS, compensation for late completion is calculated by reference to the purchase price only and not the purchase price and the contents price.

## COMMONHOLD LAND

Condition 9 of the fourth edition of the SCS has been deleted. Commonhold is not widely used as a form of tenure. Where relevant, provision for commonhold land should be made by special condition.

## CONTENTS

As previously noted, all references to 'chattels' in the SCS have been changed to 'contents'.

## FRONT AND BACK PAGES

The general layout of the front page has been changed to allow conveyancers to record on the contract cover sheet details of the exchange of contracts including the names of the respective solicitors acting for the parties, the time of exchange and the relevant formula used.

## SPECIAL CONDITIONS

### Contents and fixtures

A revised special condition 3 makes clear which contents are included in the sale and which fixtures are excluded.

### Completion

Special condition 5 allows the parties to vary condition 6.1.2 by specifying a time other than 2.00 pm in order to identify the day on which completion is to be treated as taking place for the purposes of condition 6.3 (apportionments) and 7.2 (compensation for late completion). This time will also become the earliest time for giving a notice to complete under condition 6.8.1. It is a special condition so that the parties will need to make a conscious decision if they wish to depart from the fallback provision in condition 6.1.2. It may be particularly useful where there is a chain of transactions. For example, the seller under the first contract in a chain might require payment of the purchase price by 1.30 pm to allow sufficient time to receive those funds and transmit them on his own purchase by 2.00 pm.

### Representations

The limitation on liability for representations in special condition 6 aims to exclude liability for oral statements made by or on behalf of the parties. It does not exclude liability for fraud or recklessness. The exclusion is mutual but it is most likely in practice to be relied upon by the seller. Terms similar in effect to special condition 6 are commonly found in contracts. It has been included as a special condition (rather than one of the general conditions) in the light of judicial comments in *Morgan* v. *Pooley* [2010] EWHC 2447 (QB) that the clause in that case should be given effect because it was a special condition printed in large type and easily readable.

### Occupier's consent

Special condition 7 is frequently required and has been inserted for ease of use and reference.

### E-mail service of notice

The general position under the conditions is that service by e-mail is not authorised. If the parties wish to authorise service by e-mail they will need to add an e-mail address in the space indicated at the end of the special conditions.

## APPENDIX D

# The Law Society's formulae for exchanging contracts by telephone, fax or telex[1]

**Introduction**

It is essential that an agreed memorandum of the details and of any variations of the formula used should be made at the time and retained in the file. This would be very important if any question on the exchange were raised subsequently. Agreed variations should also be confirmed in writing. The serious risks of exchanging contracts without a deposit, unless the full implications are explained to and accepted by the seller client, are demonstrated in *Morris* v. *Duke-Cohan & Co.* (1975) 119 SJ 826.

As those persons involved in the exchange will bind their firms to the undertakings in the formula used, solicitors should carefully consider who is to be authorised to exchange contracts by telephone or telex and should ensure that the use of the procedure is restricted to them. Since professional undertakings form the basis of the formulae, they are only recommended for use between firms of solicitors and licensed conveyancers.

**Law Society telephone/telex exchange – Formula A (1986)**
*(for use where one solicitor holds both signed parts of the contract):*
A completion date of [...] is agreed. The solicitor holding both parts of the contract confirms that he or she holds the part signed by his or her client(s), which is identical to the part he or she is also holding signed by the other solicitor's client(s) and will forthwith insert the agreed completion date in each part.

Solicitors mutually agree that exchange shall take place from that moment and the solicitor holding both parts confirms that, as of that moment, he or she holds the part signed by his or her client(s) to the order of the other. He or she undertakes that day by first class post, or where the other solicitor is a member of a document exchange (as to which the inclusion of a reference thereto in the solicitor's letterhead shall be conclusive evidence) by delivery to that or any other affiliated exchange, or by hand delivery direct to that solicitor's office, to send his or her signed part of the contract to the other solicitor, together, where he or she is the purchaser's solicitor, with a banker's draft or a solicitor's client account cheque for the deposit amounting to £... .

---

[1] © The Law Society. Formulae A and B: 9 July 1986, revised January 1996. Formula C: 15 March 1989, revised January 1996. The formulae were previously published in *The Guide to the Professional Conduct of Solicitors 1999* as Annex 25D.

## THE LAW SOCIETY'S FORMULAE FOR EXCHANGING CONTRACTS

*Note:*

1. *A memorandum should be prepared, after use of the formula, recording:*

    (a) *date and time of exchange;*
    (b) *the formula used and exact wording of agreed variations;*
    (c) *the completion date;*
    (d) *the (balance) deposit to be paid;*
    (e) *the identities of those involved in any conversation.*

### Law Society telephone/telex exchange – Formula B (1986)

*(for use where each solicitor holds his or her own client's signed part of the contract):*

A completion date of [...] is agreed. Each solicitor confirms to the other that he or she holds a part contract in the agreed form signed by the client(s) and will forthwith insert the agreed completion date.

Each solicitor undertakes to the other thenceforth to hold the signed part of the contract to the other's order, so that contracts are exchanged at that moment. Each solicitor further undertakes that day by first class post, or, where the other solicitor is a member of a document exchange (as to which the inclusion of a reference thereto in the solicitor's letterhead shall be conclusive evidence) by delivery to that or any other affiliated exchange, or by hand delivery direct to that solicitor's office, to send his or her signed part of the contract to the other together, in the case of a purchaser's solicitor, with a banker's draft or a solicitor's client account cheque for the deposit amounting to £....

*Notes:*

1. *A memorandum should be prepared, after use of the formula, recording:*

    (a) *date and time of exchange;*
    (b) *the formula used and exact wording of agreed variations;*
    (c) *the completion date;*
    (d) *the (balance) deposit to be paid;*
    (e) *the identities of those involved in any conversation.*

2. *Those who are going to effect the exchange must first confirm the details in order to ensure that both parts are identical. This means in particular, that if either part of the contract has been amended since it was originally prepared, the solicitor who holds a part contract with the amendments must disclose them, so that it can be confirmed that the other part is similarly amended.*

*9 July 1986, revised January 1996*

### Law Society telephone/fax/telex exchange – Formula C (1989)

Part I

The following is agreed:

Final time for exchange: [...] pm

APPENDIX D

Completion date:

Deposit to be paid to:

Each solicitor confirms that he or she holds a part of the contract in the agreed form signed by his or her client, or, if there is more than one client, by all of them. Each solicitor undertakes to the other that:

(a) he or she will continue to hold that part of the contract until the final time for exchange on the date the formula is used, and
(b) if the vendor's solicitor so notifies the purchaser's solicitor by fax, telephone or telex (whichever was previously agreed) by that time, they will both comply with part II of the formula.

The purchaser's solicitor further undertakes that either he or she or some other named person in his or her office will be available up to the final time for exchange to activate part II of the formula on receipt of the telephone call, fax or telex from the vendor's solicitors.

*Part II*

Each solicitor undertakes to the other henceforth to hold the part of the contract in his or her possession to the other's order, so that contracts are exchanged at that moment, and to despatch it to the other on that day. The purchaser's solicitor further undertakes to the vendor's solicitor to despatch on that day, or to arrange for the despatch on that day of, a banker's draft or a solicitor's client account cheque for the full deposit specified in the agreed form of contract (divided as the vendor's solicitor may have specified) to the vendor's solicitor and/or to some other solicitor whom the vendor's solicitor nominates, to be held on formula C terms.

'To despatch' means to send by first class post, or, where the other solicitor is a member of a document exchange (as to which the inclusion of a reference thereto in the solicitor's letterhead is to be conclusive evidence) by delivery to that or any other affiliated exchange, or by hand delivery direct to the recipient solicitor's office. 'Formula C terms' means that the deposit is held as stakeholder, or as agent for the vendor with authority to part with it only for the purpose of passing it to another solicitor as deposit in a related property purchase transaction on these terms.

*Notes:*

1. *Two memoranda will be required when using formula C. One needs to record the use of part I, and a second needs to record the request of the vendor's solicitor to the purchaser's solicitor to activate part II.*
2. *The first memorandum should record:*
   (a) *the date and time when it was agreed to use formula C;*
   (b) *the exact wording of any agreed variations;*
   (c) *the final time, later that day, for exchange;*
   (d) *the completion date;*
   (e) *the name of the solicitor to whom the deposit was to be paid, or details of amounts and names if it was to be split; and*
   (f) *the identities of those involved in any conversation.*
3. *Formula C assumes the payment of a full contractual deposit (normally 10%).*
4. *The contract term relating to the deposit must allow it to be passed on, with payment direct from payer to ultimate recipient, in the way in which the*

formula contemplates. The deposit must ultimately be held by a solicitor as stakeholder. Whilst some variation in the formula can be agreed this is a term of the formula which must not be varied, unless all the solicitors involved in the chain have agreed.

5. If a buyer proposes to use a deposit guarantee policy, formula C will need substantial adaptation.

6. It is essential prior to agreeing part I of formula C that those effecting the exchange ensure that both parts of the contract are identical.

7. Using formula C involves a solicitor in giving a number of professional undertakings. These must be performed precisely. Any failure will be a serious breach of professional discipline. One of the undertakings may be to arrange that someone over whom the solicitor has no control will do something (i.e. to arrange for someone else to despatch the cheque or banker's draft in payment of the deposit). An undertaking is still binding even if it is to do something outside the solicitor's control.

8. Solicitors do not as a matter of law have an automatic authority to exchange contracts on a formula C basis, and should always ensure that they have the client's express authority to use formula C. A suggested form of authority is set out below. It should be adapted to cover any special circumstances:

I/We [...] understand that my/our sale and purchase of [...] are both part of a chain of linked property transactions, in which all parties want the security of contracts which become binding on the same day.

I/We agree that you should make arrangements with the other solicitors or licensed conveyancers involved to achieve this.

I/We understand that this involves each property-buyer offering, early on one day, to exchange contracts whenever, later that day, the seller so requests, and that the buyer's offer is on the basis that it cannot be withdrawn or varied during that day.

I/We agree that when I/we authorise you to exchange contracts, you may agree to exchange contracts on the above basis and give any necessary undertakings to the other parties involved in the chain and that my/our authority to you cannot be revoked throughout the day on which the offer to exchange contracts is made.

*15 March 1989, revised January 1996*

# APPENDIX E

# The Law Society Code for Completion by Post[1]

**Warning: Use of this code embodies professional undertakings.**

See SRA Warning Card on Undertakings.

See also 'Accepting undertakings on completion following the Court of Appeal decision in *Patel* v. *Daybells*' (Appendix IV.6 of the 17th edition *Conveyancing Handbook*). [Appendix I of this book.]

## INTRODUCTION AND SCOPE

The code provides a voluntary procedure for postal completion for residential transactions. It may also be used by licensed conveyancers. Solicitors adopting the code must be satisfied that its adoption will not be contrary to the interests of their client. When adopted, the code applies without variation unless otherwise agreed.

It is intended to provide a fair balance of obligation between seller's and buyer's solicitors and to facilitate professional co-operation for the benefit of clients.

## PROCEDURE

### General

1. To adopt this code, both solicitors must agree, preferably in writing, to use it to complete a specific transaction, except that the use or adoption of the Law Society Conveyancing Protocol automatically implies use of this code unless otherwise stated in writing by either solicitor.
2. If the seller's solicitor has to withdraw from using the code, the buyer's solicitor should be notified of this not later than 4pm on the working day prior to the completion date. If the seller's solicitor's authority to receive the monies is withdrawn later the buyer's solicitor must be notified immediately.
3. In complying with the terms of the code, the seller's solicitor acts on completion as the buyer's solicitor's agent without fee or disbursement but this obligation does not require

---

[1] © The Law Society 2011.

the seller's solicitor to investigate or take responsibility for any breach of the seller's contractual obligations and is expressly limited to completion pursuant to paragraphs 10 to 12.

**Before completion**

4. The buyer's solicitor will use reasonable endeavours to ensure that sufficient funds are collected from the buyer and any mortgage lender in good time to transmit to the seller's solicitor on or before the completion date.
5. The seller's solicitor should provide to the buyer's solicitor replies to completion information and undertakings in the Law Society's standard form at least five working days before the completion date unless replies have been provided to such other form requesting completion information as may have been submitted by the buyer's solicitor.
6. The seller's solicitor will specify in writing to the buyer's solicitor the mortgages, charges or other financial incumbrances secured on the property which on or before completion are to be redeemed or discharged to the extent that they relate to the property, and by what method.
7. The seller's solicitor **undertakes**:

    (i) to have the seller's authority to receive the purchase money on completion; and
    (ii) on completion, to have the authority of the proprietor of each mortgage, charge or other financial incumbrance which was specified under paragraph 6 but has not then been redeemed or discharged, to receive the sum intended to repay it;

    **BUT** if the seller's solicitor does not have all the necessary authorities then:
    (iii) to advise the buyer's solicitor no later than 4pm on the working day before the completion date of the absence of those authorities or immediately if any is withdrawn later; and
    (iv) not to complete without the buyer's solicitor's instructions.

8. The buyer's solicitor may send the seller's solicitor instructions as to any other matters required by the buyer's solicitor which may include:

    (i) documents to be examined and marked;
    (ii) memoranda to be endorsed;
    (iii) undertakings to be given;
    (iv) deeds or other documents including transfers and any relevant undertakings and authorities relating to rents, deposits, keys, to be sent to the buyer's solicitor following completion;
    (v) consents, certificates or other authorities that may be required to deal with any restrictions on any Land Registry title to the property;
    (vi) executed Stock Transfer Forms relating to shares in any companies directly related to the conveyancing transaction.

9. The buyer's solicitor will remit to the seller's solicitor the sum required to complete, as notified in writing on the seller's solicitor's completion statement or otherwise in accordance with the contract, including any compensation payable for late completion by reference to the 'contract rate' if the Standard Conditions of Sale are utilised, or in default of notification as shown by the contract. If the funds are remitted by transfer between banks, immediately upon becoming aware of their receipt, the seller's solicitor will report to the buyer's solicitor that the funds have been received.

APPENDIX E

**Completion**

10. The seller's solicitor will complete upon becoming aware of the receipt of the sum specified in paragraph 9, or a lesser sum should the buyer's and seller's solicitors so agree, unless –

    (i) the buyer's solicitor has notified the seller's solicitor that the funds are to be held to the buyer's solicitor's order; or
    (ii) it has previously been agreed that completion takes place at a later time.

    Any agreement or notification under this paragraph should if possible be made or confirmed in writing.

11. When completing, the seller's solicitor **undertakes**:

    (i) to comply with any agreed completion arrangements and any reasonable instructions given under paragraph 8;
    (ii) to redeem or obtain discharges for every mortgage, charge or other financial incumbrance specified under paragraph 6 so far as it relates to the property which has not already been redeemed or discharged;
    (iii) that the proprietor of each mortgage, charge or other financial incumbrance specified under paragraph 6 has been identified by the seller's solicitor to the extent necessary for the purpose of the buyer's solicitor's application to HM Land Registry.

**After completion**

12. The seller's solicitor **undertakes**:

    (i) immediately completion has taken place to hold to the buyer's solicitor's order every document specified under paragraph 8 and not to exercise a lien over any of them;
    (ii) as soon as possible after completion, and in any event on the same day:

        (a) to confirm to the buyer's solicitor by telephone, fax or email that completion has taken place;
        (b) to notify the seller's estate agent or other keyholder that completion has taken place and authorise them to make keys available to the buyer immediately;

    (iii) as soon as possible after completion and in any event by the end of the working day following completion to send written confirmation and, at the risk of the buyer's solicitor, the items specified under paragraph 8 to the buyer's solicitor by first class post or document exchange;
    (iv) if the discharge of any mortgage, charge or other financial incumbrance specified under paragraph 6 takes place by electronic means, to notify the buyer's solicitor as soon as confirmation is received from the proprietor of the mortgage, charge or other financial encumbrance that the discharge has taken or is taking place.

**Supplementary**

13. The rights and obligations of the parties, under the contract or otherwise, are not affected by this code and in the event of a conflict between the contract and this code, the contract shall prevail.

14. (i) References to the seller's solicitor and the buyer's solicitor apply as appropriate to solicitors acting for other parties who adopt the code.

(ii) When a licensed conveyancer adopts this code, references to a solicitor include a licensed conveyancer.
15. A dispute or difference arising between solicitors who adopt this code (whether or not subject to any variation) relating directly to its application is to be referred to a single arbitrator agreed between the solicitors. If they do not agree on the appointment within one month, the President of the Law Society may appoint the arbitrator at the request of one of the solicitors.

**NOTES TO THE CODE**

1. This code will apply to transactions where the code is adopted after the first day of April 2011.
2. The object of this code is to provide solicitors with a convenient means for completion on an agency basis when a representative of the buyer's solicitor is not attending at the office of the seller's solicitor.
3. As with the Law Society's formulae for exchange of contracts, the code embodies professional undertakings and is only recommended for adoption between solicitors and licensed conveyancers.
4. Paragraph 3 of the code provides that the seller's solicitor will act as agent for the buyer's solicitor without fee or disbursements. The convenience of not having to make a specific appointment on the date of completion for the buyer's solicitor to attend to complete personally will offset the agency work that the seller's solicitor has to do and any postage payable in completing under the code. Most solicitors will from time to time act for both sellers and buyers. If a seller's solicitor does consider that charges and/or disbursements are necessary in a particular case this would represent a variation in the code and should be agreed in writing before exchange of contracts.
5. In view of the decision in *Edward Wong Finance Company Limited* v. *Johnson, Stokes and Master* [1984] AC 296, clause 7(ii) of the code requires the seller's solicitor to undertake on completion to have the authority of the proprietor of every mortgage or charge to be redeemed to receive the sum needed to repay such charge. Such an undertaking remains an indispensable component of residential conveyancing. While the seller's solicitor will often not be specifically instructed by the seller's mortgagee, the course of dealings between the solicitor and mortgagee in relation to the monies required to redeem the mortgage should at the very least evidence implicit authority from the mortgagee to the solicitor to receive the sum required to repay the charge (if, for example, the mortgagee has given its bank details to the solicitor for transmission of the redemption funds).

On the basis of those dealings (and in the absence of any contrary statements from the mortgagee), the seller's solicitor should be in a position to give the undertaking to discharge (in the Law Society's recommended form, adapted where relevant for electronic discharges) and, for paper discharges (DS1, etc.), to undertake that they have identified the seller's mortgagee to the extent necessary for the purpose of the buyer's solicitor's application to the Land Registry, on which the buyer's solicitor should be able to rely.

The seller's solicitor should, if at all possible, receive an express confirmation from the seller's mortgagee that the paper discharge, or an acknowledgment of discharge (for electronic discharges) will be supplied to them. If the seller's mortgagee expressly prohibits the seller's solicitor from dealing with the redemption money, the seller's solicitor should notify the buyer's solicitor as soon as possible. The seller's solicitor and buyer's solicitor should consider whether in those circumstances they can adopt the code and, if so, the necessary variations.

APPENDIX E

6. In view of the decisions in *Angel Solicitors (a firm)* v. *Jenkins O'Dowd & Barth* http://www.bailii.org/ew/cases/EWHC/Ch/2009/46.html and *Clark* v. *Lucas LLP* [2009] EWHC 1952 (Ch) the undertaking in clause 11(ii) of this code is to be taken, unless otherwise stated, as including confirmation that a satisfactory redemption statement has been obtained from the lender whose charge is to be redeemed.
7. Paragraph 13 of the code provides that nothing in the code shall override any rights and obligations of the parties under the contract or otherwise.
8. The seller's solicitor is to inform the buyer's solicitor of the mortgages or charges which will be redeemed or discharged (see paragraph 6 of the code). The information may be given in reply to completion information and undertakings (see paragraph 5 of the code). Such a reply may also amount to an undertaking.
9. Care must be taken if there is a sale and sub-sale. The sub-seller's solicitors may not hold the transfer nor be in a position to receive the funds required to discharge the seller's mortgage on the property. Enquiries should be made to ascertain if the monies or some of the monies payable on completion should, with the authority of either the sub-seller or the sub-seller's solicitor, be sent direct to the seller's solicitor and not to the sub-seller's solicitor.
10. Care must also be taken if there is a simultaneous resale and completion and enquiries should be made by the ultimate buyer's solicitor of the intermediate seller's solicitor as to the price being paid on that purchase. Having appointed the intermediate seller's solicitor as agent the buyer's solicitor is fixed with the knowledge of an agent even without having personal knowledge (see the SRA Warning Card on Property Fraud).
11. For the purposes of paragraphs 9 and 10 (of the code) as it will be in the best interests of the client to know as soon as possible that completion has taken place it is assumed that procedures promptly to notify the arrival of monies will be in place.

These notes refer only to some of the points in the code that practitioners may wish to consider before agreeing to adopt it. Any variation in the code must be agreed in writing before the completion date.

# APPENDIX F

# Certificate of title

**ANNEX**

**CERTIFICATE OF TITLE**

**Details box**

| |
|---|
| TO: (Lender) |
| Lender's Reference or Account No: |
| The Borrower: |
| Property: |
| Title Number: |
| Mortgage Advance: |
| Price stated in transfer: |
| Completion Date: |
| Conveyancer's Name & Address: |
| Conveyancer's Reference: |
| Conveyancer's bank, sort code and account number: |
| Date of instructions: |

**WE THE CONVEYANCERS NAMED ABOVE CERTIFY** as follows:

(1) If so instructed, we have checked the identity of the Borrower (and anyone else required to sign the mortgage deed or other document connected with the mortgage) by reference to the document or documents precisely specified in writing by you.

(2) Except as otherwise disclosed to you in writing:

    (i) we have investigated the title to the Property, we are not aware of any other financial charges secured on the Property which will affect the Property after completion of the mortgage and, upon completion of the mortgage, both you and the mortgagor (whose identity has been checked in accordance with paragraph (1) above) will have a good and marketable title to the Property and to appurtenant rights free from prior mortgages or charges and from onerous encumbrances which title will be registered with absolute title;

    (ii) we have compared the extent of the Property shown on any plan provided by you against relevant plans in the title deeds and/or the description of the

APPENDIX F

        Property in any valuation which you have supplied to us, and in our opinion there are no material discrepancies;
- (iii) the assumptions stated by the valuer about the title (its tenure, easements, boundaries and restrictions on use) in any valuation which you have supplied to us are correct;
- (iv) if the Property is leasehold the terms of the lease accord with your instructions, including any requirements you have for covenants by the Landlord and/or a management company and/or by a deed of mutual covenant for the insurance, repair and maintenance of the structure, exterior and common parts of any building of which the Property forms part, and we have or will obtain on or before completion a clear receipt for the last payment of rent and service charge;
- (v) if the Property is a commonhold unit, the commonhold community statement contains the terms specified by you and does not include any restrictions on occupation or use specified by you as unacceptable, and we have or will obtain on or before completion a commonhold unit information certificate;
- (vi) we have received satisfactory evidence that the buildings insurance is in place, or will be on completion, for the sum and in the terms required by you;
- (vii) if the Property is to be purchased by the Borrower:
  - (a) the contract for sale provides for vacant possession on completion;
  - (b) the seller has owned or been the registered owner of the Property for not less than six months; and
  - (c) we are not acting on behalf of the seller;
- (viii) we are in possession of:
  - (a) either a local search or local search insurance; and
  - (b) such other searches or search insurance as are appropriate to the Property, the mortgagor and any guarantor, in each case in accordance with your instructions;
- (ix) nothing has been revealed by our searches and enquiries which would prevent the Property being used by any occupant for residential purposes; and
- (x) neither any principal nor any other individual in the firm giving this certificate nor any spouse, child, parent, brother or sister of such a person is interested in the Property (whether alone or jointly with any other) as mortgagor.

**WE:**

- (a) undertake, prior to use of the mortgage advance, to obtain in the form required by you the execution of a mortgage and a guarantee as appropriate by the persons whose identities have been checked in accordance with paragraph (1) above as those of the Borrower, any other person in whom the legal estate is vested and any guarantor; and, if required by you:
  - (i) to obtain their signatures to the forms of undertaking required by you in relation to the use, occupation or physical state of the Property;
  - (ii) to ask the Borrower for confirmation that the information about occupants given in your mortgage instructions or offer is correct; and
  - (iii) to obtain consents in the form required by you from any existing or prospective occupier(s) aged 17 or over of the Property specified by you or of whom we are aware;
- (b) have made or will make such Bankruptcy, Land Registry or Land Charges Searches as may be necessary to justify certificate no. (2)(i) above;

# CERTIFICATE OF TITLE

(c) will within the period of protection afforded by the searches referred to in paragraph (b) above:

    (i) complete the mortgage;
    (ii) arrange for the issue of a stamp duty land tax certificate if appropriate;
    (iii) deliver to the Land Registry the documents necessary to register the mortgage in your favour and any relevant prior dealings; and
    (iv) effect any other registrations necessary to protect your interests as mortgagee;

(d) will despatch to you such deeds and documents relating to the Property as you require with a list of them in the form prescribed by you within ten working days of receipt by us of the title information document from the Land Registry;

(e) will not part with the mortgage advance (and will return it to you if required) if it shall come to our notice prior to completion that the Property will at completion be occupied in whole or in part otherwise than in accordance with your instructions;

(f) will not accept instructions, except with your consent in writing, to prepare any lease or tenancy agreement relating to the Property or any part of it prior to despatch of the title information document to you;

(g) will not use the mortgage advance until satisfied that, prior to or contemporaneously with the transfer of the Property to the mortgagor, there will be discharged:

    (i) any existing mortgage on property the subject of an associated sale of which we are aware; and
    (ii) any other mortgages made by a lender identified by you secured against a property located in England or Wales where you have given either an account number or numbers or a property address;

(h) will notify you in writing if any matter comes to our attention before completion which would render the certificate given above untrue or inaccurate and, in those circumstances, will defer completion pending your authority to proceed and will return the mortgage advance to you if required; and

(i) confirm that we have complied, or will comply, with your instructions in all other respects to the extent that they do not extend beyond the limitations contained in the Solicitors' Code of Conduct 2007, 3.19 (Conflict of interests – types of instruction which may be accepted).

**OUR** duties to you are limited to the matters set out in this certificate and we accept no further liability or responsibility whatsoever. The payment by you to us (by whatever means) of the mortgage advance or any part of it constitutes acceptance of this limitation and any assignment to you by the Borrower of any rights of action against us to which the Borrower may be entitled shall take effect subject to this limitation.

**Signature box**

| SIGNED on behalf of THE CONVEYANCERS: |
|---|
| NAME of Authorised Signatory: |
| QUALIFICATION of Authorised Signatory: |
| DATE of Signature: |

## APPENDIX G(I)

# Warning Card on Property Fraud[1]

**The Solicitors Regulation Authority will not tolerate property fraud.**

Your obligations are set out in rules 1, 2, 3, 4 and 18 of the Solicitors' Code of Conduct 2007 and its guidance.

### If in doubt – refuse to act

You must ensure that you do not facilitate dubious property transactions. Failure to observe our warnings could lead to disciplinary action or criminal prosecution.

If you doubt the propriety of a transaction you should refuse to act. Ensure you verify and question instructions to satisfy yourself that you are not facilitating a dubious transaction.

### What is property fraud?

Mortgage fraud occurs when a loan is obtained on the basis of untrue statements to the lender, such as when a lender is led to believe that a property is worth more than its true value and therefore lends more than it would if it knew the true position. Always focus on informing the lender of the true price and other relevant facts, while taking into account confidentiality and legal professional privilege.

Some frauds do not involve a mortgage – only the deception of buyers.

### Warning signs

- Back-to-back transactions where a property is bought and then sold quickly, apparently at a higher price. The lender advances money based on the higher price
- Misrepresentation or changes to the purchase price including sellers or developers providing incentives, allowances or discounts unless these are clearly and fully disclosed to the lender
- A representation to you that a deposit or part of the purchase price is paid direct
- 'Gifted deposit' or 'deposit paid' by the seller amounting to a reduction in the price paid by the buyer but distorting the value disclosed to the lender
- Unusual or suspicious instructions such as transactions controlled or funded by a third party; a client using an alias; sales and purchases between associates; parties using the same legal adviser; a request that net proceeds be sent to a third party

---

[1] © The Law Society 2009. Last updated by the Solicitors Regulation Authority April 2009.

- Properties sold between related offshore or corporate companies that are commonly controlled by the same individuals, particularly where the properties are mortgaged at an inflated value

Be aware that variations of these warning signs exist and fraudsters change their methods. You do not need to act for the lender to become implicated. If you are not satisfied of the propriety of the transaction you should refuse to act.

**Money laundering**

Bear in mind that you may also have legal obligations to report your suspicions to the Serious Organised Crime Agency (SOCA).

For good-practice advice, refer to www.lawsociety.org.uk/mortgagefraud.

To report to us on a confidential basis, contact our Fraud and Confidential Intelligence Bureau on 01926 439673 or 0845 850 0999 or email redalert@sra.org.uk.

For conduct advice, contact our Professional Ethics helpline.

## APPENDIX G(II)

# Warning Card on Money Laundering[1]

**The Solicitors Regulation Authority is determined to pursue those it regulates who are involved in money laundering.**

Your obligations are set out in the Solicitors' Code of Conduct 2007, particularly rules 1 and 4, the Solicitors' Accounts Rules, the Proceeds of Crime Act 2002, the Terrorism Act 2000, and the Money Laundering Regulations 2007.

You must ensure that you do not facilitate laundering even when money does not pass though your firm's accounts. Failure to observe our warnings can lead to disciplinary action, criminal prosecution, or both.

**Warning signs**

*Unusual payment requests*

- Payments from a third party where you cannot verify the source of the funds
- Receipts of cash and requests for payments by cash
- Money transfers where there is a variation between the account holder/signatory
- Payments to unrelated third parties
- Litigation settlements which are reached too easily.

*Unusual instructions*

- Instructions outside the normal pattern of your business
- Instructions changed without a reasonable explanation
- Transactions that take an unusual turn
- Movement of funds between accounts, institutions or jurisdictions without reason.

*Use of your client account*

- Never accept instructions to act as a banking facility, particularly if you do not undertake any related legal work – be aware of note (ix) to rule 15 of the Solicitors' Accounts Rules 1998
- Be wary if you are instructed to do legal work, receive substantial funds into your client account, but the instructions are later cancelled and you are asked to send the money to a third party or perhaps to your client.

---

[1] © The Law Society 2009. Last updated by the Solicitors Regulation Authority April 2009.

# WARNING CARD ON MONEY LAUNDERING

*Suspect territory*

- Check official sources about suspect territories and sanctions.
- Be wary of funds moved around without a logical explanation.

*Loss making transaction*

- Instructions potentially leading to financial loss without logical explanation, particularly where your client seems unconcerned.

Legislation may require you to make an official disclosure to the Serious Organised Crime Agency (SOCA), PO Box 8000, London, SE11 5EN, call 020 7238 8282, or send an email by registering on the secure site at www.ukciu.gov.uk/saroline.aspx. You will not commit the offence of 'tipping off' by reporting a matter to the SRA. To report to us on a confidential basis, contact our Fraud and Confidential Intelligence Bureau on 01926 439673 or 0845 850 0999 or email redalert@sra.org.uk.

For conduct advice, contact our Professional Ethics helpline.

For general queries about good-practice anti-money laundering compliance, contact the Law Society's Practice Advice Service on 0870 606 2522 (9:00-17:00 Monday to Friday) or refer to **www.lawsociety.org.uk/moneylaundering**

## APPENDIX G(III)

# Warning Card on Undertakings[1]

**The SRA takes breaches of undertakings very seriously.**

Your obligations are set out in rules 1, 5.01 and 10.05 of the Solicitors' Code of Conduct 2007 and its guidance.

Many transactions depend on the use of undertakings enabling you to negotiate and conduct your client's business successfully.

**Where you give an undertaking**

Those placing reliance on it will expect you to fulfil it. Ensure your undertakings are:
- Specific
- Measurable
- Agreed
- Realistic
- Timed

A breach of undertaking can lead to a disciplinary finding and costs direction.

Undertakings you give are also summarily enforceable by the High Court. Be aware that you do not become exposed to a liability within the excess of your firm's insurance.

**Where you accept an undertaking**

Ensure that in doing so your client's position is protected and you are not exposed to a breach.

**If you are a regulated person or firm**

- Be clear about who can give undertakings.
- Ensure all staff understand they need your client's agreement.
- Be clear about how compliance will be monitored.
- Maintain a central record to ensure and monitor compliance.
- Prescribe the manner in which undertakings may be given.
- Prepare standard undertakings, where possible, with clear instructions that any departure be authorised in accordance with supervision and management responsibilities.
- Adopt a system that ensures terms are checked by another fee-earner.

---

[1] © The Law Society 2009. Last updated by the Solicitors Regulation Authority April 2009.

## WARNING CARD ON UNDERTAKINGS

- Confirm oral undertakings (given or received) in writing.
- Copy each undertaking and attach it to the relevant file; label the file itself.
- Ensure all staff understand the undertakings they give when using the Law Society's formulae for exchange of contracts and its code for completion by post.

To report to us on a confidential basis, contact our Fraud and Confidential Intelligence Bureau on 01926 439673 or 0845 850 0999 or email redalert@sra.org.uk.

For advice, contact our Professional Ethics helpline.

## APPENDIX H(I)

# Land Registry early completion practice note[1]

## 1 INTRODUCTION

### 1.1 Who should read this practice note?

Solicitors dealing with conveyancing matters for buyers, sellers and lenders.

### 1.2 What is the issue?

From 3 August 2009, Land Registry (LR) will introduce 'early completion'. The early completion policy will apply to any situation involving a discharge of whole and another application. This new process relates to the procedure for, and the order in which LR will process multiple applications including discharge of a seller's charge.

Applications containing such multiple requests will be treated as separate applications. For example this means that where applications to discharge a seller's charge, transfer title to the buyer, then register the buyer's charge are made together, but evidence of discharge does not accompany the application and has not already been received by LR, LR will complete registration of the other applications, where possible.

This will leave the entries relating to existing charge(s) subsisting in the register. A transfer to a buyer and the buyer's charge might be registered before a seller's charge is removed from the title. Early completion may apply regardless of the method of discharge being used by the seller's lender.

Crucially, LR early completion does not mean legal or physical completion of the transaction. It simply means acceleration of when LR will make the first changes to the register in connection with the applications received. This practice note gives advice on:

- how early completion will operate
- handling applications where the registered proprietor's charge contains a restriction
- how to proceed with the different applications
- undertakings
- discharges
- identification
- fees.

---

[1] © The Law Society. This practice note is as stated on 9 July 2009. Practice notes are updated by the Law Society from time to time. Solicitors are advised to check **www.lawsociety.org.uk** for the latest version.

LAND REGISTRY EARLY COMPLETION PRACTICE NOTE

## 2   THE ESTABLISHED PROCEDURE ON SALE

LR currently treat applications to discharge the seller's charge, transfer to the buyer and add the buyer's charge as linked and conditional upon each other. They are dealt with in that order.

So until evidence of discharge of the seller's charge is available to LR and has been registered, all of the applications are held over, except where the discharge takes place by ED or e-DS1.

LR allow applications like this to be held over several times, awaiting proof of satisfaction of a charge if you do all of the following:

- make a request for an extension of time
- keep LR informed as to progress
- show that you are actively pursuing the matter
- show that the lender is causing the delay.

LR consider requests for further extensions of time beyond an initial 20 business day period on their merits. Such extensions are granted largely when LR think it is realistic that the discharge will be produced in a reasonable time.

The applications to discharge, transfer and charge are likely to be cancelled, if:

- it appears unlikely that the discharge will be produced in a reasonable time
- you are not able to explain the reason for the delay or what is being done to obtain proof of satisfaction of the charge.

Provided that LR receive your application before 3 August 2009 it will be processed under the established procedure; LR will requisition for a discharge if this is not lodged before or with the application.

## 3   EARLY COMPLETION FROM 3 AUGUST 2009

Early completion will apply when you make an application to register (for example, for a sale remortgage or lease) that accompanies an application to discharge an existing charge of whole, and proof of satisfaction of that charge does not accompany or precede the application.

When you make an application like this, LR will reject the application for discharge, but will complete the other applications, where possible. The entries relating to the existing charge will be left on the register until LR receive proof of satisfaction of repayment of the mortgage.

How LR deal with the application will depend upon whether or not a restriction is registered in favour of the existing chargee.

### 3.1   Sellers' charges without restrictions

Early completion will operate immediately where the seller's charge does not contain matters on which requisitions need to be raised. The registrations will happen in the order that complete applications are received by LR, subject to the effect of any priority search. Complete applications are those that are ready to be processed with no documents missing or to follow.

If there are matters on which requisitions need to be raised LR will include a reminder about the missing discharge in their requisition but the missing discharge will not be a point on which a requisition is raised.

APPENDIX H(l)

This may result in the transfer and the new charge being registered without the prior charge being removed.

### 3.2 Sellers' charges containing a restriction

When acting for a buyer, you should establish any relevant restrictions early in the transaction from the proprietorship register. This is prudent because the content of the restriction on the register will determine how LR will apply the new policy.

Restrictions in favour of a proprietor's chargees may prevent the registration of any further charge or in most cases of any disposition without the chargee's written consent. In such cases, the LR will requisition for either:

- proof of satisfaction of the charge
- evidence of compliance with the restriction.

If the lender does not provide evidence of the discharge within twenty business days, you will not be able to address the requisition within that time. In these circumstances, the LR will allow a further twenty business day extension if you do all of the following:

- make a written request for the extension
- demonstrate that you are actively pursuing the matter
- show that the existing lender is causing the delay.

LR has not given further formal guidance on these requirements. We assume that they will operate as before 3 August 2009 if you are unable to satisfy the requisition within the time limit.

LR will cancel both your application for discharge and applications to register the transfer and charge, where there is a restriction against the registration of any disposition. This time limit is up to forty business days if you have successfully applied for an extension. At the expiration of the time limit the application will be cancelled. LR will allow less time for satisfying any requisitions under early completion.

It may be of some benefit to make an additional priority search immediately prior to legal completion to extend the initial time available within which to obtain the evidence of discharge.

In the rarer case of a restriction only against the registration of charges, LR will complete the registration of the transfer, and cancel the application for discharge, which will leave the existing charge entries on the register. LR will also cancel the application for the new charge. The face of the register will then show the buyer as registered proprietor and the seller's lender as the mortgagee.

### 3.3 If your application is cancelled

As now, if your application is cancelled, you might lose priority for the application, unless you re-submit it within the priority period and it is subsequently registered.

Unless the further application is made within any existing priority period, priority for the interest will be lost if there is any competing application and/or search made before you made a further application to register the disposition, or received a further clear search. Making a further search will give you a new priority period, not extend the original one. The new search cannot act retrospectively and attach itself to the substantive application already lodged.

As is the case currently, the application will be subject to any other application or search made in respect of the property before your new search takes effect. If, for example, a further search is made at the time an extension is requested, whilst it will remain in the LR day list for thirty business days, it will not provide protection for the pending application. The application will have priority by virtue of it having been lodged at LR and entered in the day list. This means that from day thirty, when your search expires, to day 40, when your extension expires, the application will have priority by virtue of its entry in the day list and not by virtue of your search.

The new search may provide priority for any renewed application but this will depend on whether any other search and/or applications have been lodged before the search is received by LR.

Where there is a restriction and either early completion has been applied or LR has cancelled applications because of failure to satisfy a requisition, any official search protecting the cancelled application will remain in effect until its expiry.

### 3.4 Following the first part of the registration process

To avoid early completion leaving sellers' or outgoing charges on the register for a long time after completion of other parts of the registration, you should do both of the following:

1. Check the Registration Completion Sheet (RCS) letter you receive from LR to understand the status of the registration and to establish whether you should make further applications to conclude the necessary registration, particularly in relation to cancelling the seller's charge.
2. Establish office procedures to monitor the status of recently made and completed applications.

LR will make it very clear on the RCS where registration has been completed on the basis of early completion, and what other steps should be taken depending on the nature of the application. LR is currently developing the proposed wording.

### 3.5 The further application for registration of the discharge

*3.5.1 Discharge by DS1*

Where you are awaiting a paper DS1 you should make your subsequent application for registration of the discharge when you receive the DS1 from the seller's lender or seller's solicitor.

*3.5.2 Discharge by Electronic Notification of Discharge (END)*

ENDs do not incorporate an application to register, so you will need to establish if the END is available before making your second application in form AP1 or DS2E for the charge entries to be cancelled.

Lenders should notify the seller's solicitor, who will usually be redeeming the seller's charge, when they have sent an END to LR. The seller's solicitors in most cases will not be making application to redeem the seller's charge. You, the buyer's solicitor, will usually be making this application. This is why it is important that the sellers' solicitors immediately pass such information or notification as they receive from the lender to you. Some lenders, in relation to some electronic methods of discharge, provide no further notification following the redemption statement.

You can make a day list enquiry of LR to find out if an END transmitted by the lender is awaiting registration or view the register to find out whether the charge has been removed electronically.

Alternatively you can phone the relevant local LR office to establish that:

APPENDIX H(I)

- the charge entries have been cancelled following receipt of an ED or e-DS1
- an END, ED or e-DS1 has been received, or
- no END, ED or e-DS1 has been received.

This is a free service.

You can also contact LR telephone services centre to make an END enquiry. Call 0844 892 0307 for properties in England and 0844 892 0308 for properties in Wales and for the Welsh speaking service.

*3.5.3 Restrictions against the registration of charges*

In the case of a restriction against the registration of charges rather than against any disposition, LR will register the transfer and then requisition as set out in 3.2 above. If LR then receive the discharge LR will register this and subsequently register the buyer's charge which will be part of the application they are already holding provided that time limits have not been exceeded and the application has not been cancelled. This applies to discharges by both DS1 and END.

*3.5.4 Discharge by ED and E-DS1*

Both of these kinds of electronic discharge incorporate an application to LR to discharge the charge. You therefore do not need to make any further application to LR to register the discharge but to comply with your obligations you do need to monitor the status of the original application.

**3.6 Title Information Documents (TIDs)**

A TID will be issued as usual following completion of a registration. LR will issue the RCS and the TID which includes an official copy of the register.

LR will issue a TID and an official copy of the register after the subsequent application.

LR are considering the following issues:

- whether and how notification should be sent to you when a charge left on the register after early completion is subsequently discharged by an ED or a e-DS1.
- whether any such notification should also include an updated official copy of the register.

**3.7 Lenders' checking of the register**

Lenders are likely to continue to make checks to establish when applications for registrations have been made following a purchase and whether they were they made within the priority period. Once early completion is introduced, lenders are likely to want to know whether they have a registered first charge and whether any former charges have been removed from the register. The fact that lenders may be carrying out these checks does not relieve you of your duty to the lender to make your own checks.

**4 COUNCIL OF MORTGAGE LENDERS (CML) HANDBOOK**

The CML Handbook states that on completion of the instructions in a retainer, the lender will require a fully enforceable first legal charge. The CML say this requirement remains unchanged by LR's early completion processes. The CML's view is that early completion is not an issue substantially affecting the current process. Accordingly they do not propose to amend the Handbook.

The CML states:

> The order of events may in some cases be reversed but the stages of the process remain exactly the same.
> Lenders regard completion as having taken place once the retainer is complied with. It is not relevant that the Land Registry has imposed an intervening stage in the transaction as this does not change the overall position.

By 'completion', the CML means completion of the instructions from a lender, not legal or physical completion.

In connection with the CML Handbook LR states that:

> Completing the applications to register the transfer and new charge subject to the existing charge would not appear to affect the obligations of any party in relation to that existing charge. If the existing charge has been repaid then the requirement on the lender to provide evidence of proof of satisfaction of that charge will remain. The obligation of the seller's conveyancer arising from any undertaking given to the buyer's conveyancer in relation to the charge will not change.
> Early completion will not prevent the new charge taking effect as a first legal charge; it can never become a first charge until the existing charge is discharged. This is so whether or not the new charge is entered in the register. The entry of the new charge under early completion simply protects the priority of that new charge as against any other interest whose priority is not protected at the time of registration.

The CML states that the changes will not alter the requirements set out in paragraph 14.1.1.1 of the CML Lenders Handbook which require the conveyancer to register the mortgage as a first legal charge at the Land Registry. Lenders do not regard the retainer as being complied with until this is achieved.

By implication this suggests that lenders will not regard the temporary situation, of the buyer's mortgagee having a second mortgage whilst the seller's mortgage is awaiting discharge, as being in breach of the provisions of the CML Handbook. This is so because lenders will not regard completion as having taken place until the retainer has been completed by the lender being registered with a first legal charge. It is upon completion of, and not during, the retainer, that lenders require a first legal charge.

## 5 UNDERTAKINGS AND ASSURANCES

Early completion is a policy change that does not directly affect the existing advice in the *Conveyancing Handbook* and Rule 10 of the Code of Conduct in relation to undertakings.

The changes in practice arising from early completion may make you, as a buyer's solicitor, want to seek further assurances from the seller's solicitor. You may seek these by way of representations, contractual obligations and/or undertakings.

Where you seek a further or extended undertaking to meet the requirements of the early completion policy, the seller's solicitor will need to consider whether any such extended undertaking can properly be given. It may not be possible, or proper for the seller's solicitor to give such extended undertaking.

In order to attempt to meet the requirements of early completion you may instead seek pre-contract representations or warranties from the seller's solicitors that they will:

APPENDIX H(1)

- pay over the money required to discharge the charge on completion
- press the lender for the discharge
- endeavour to obtain from the lender and will supply to the buyer information about the likely method of discharge to be used
- in the absence of DS1, DS3 or END notices continue to press for such information and supply such information as is available to them as to the status and likely issue time of the release.

Note carefully that a 'representation' or 'warranty' to do something could well amount to an undertaking (see Solicitors' Code of Conduct rule 10.05 and the associated guidance).

These assurances may assist in providing you with the necessary information to enable you to apply to the LR for extensions of time or to make further priority searches. However, even if the seller's solicitor provides full information this will not resolve the problem. If the discharge is not available within the extended time limits the application is likely to be rejected, but the information you receive may assist you in assessing the risk of this occurring in any transaction.

Making a further priority search does not guarantee protection. Making a further search will give you a new priority period; it will not extend the original one. The search result will be subject to any other application or search made in respect of the property before your new search takes effect. In these circumstances you will be acting in your clients' interest by requesting and obtaining such assurances from the seller's solicitor to ensure that priority for the buyer's registration of ownership and the lenders registration of charge is protected.

Solicitors acting for sellers can reasonably be expected to co-operate in affording such information and assurances as are reasonable as this will, in most cases, be in their own clients 'best interests.'

For further information on conveyancing undertakings to discharge mortgages see both:

1. rule 10.05 of the Solicitors' Code of Conduct
2. the *Conveyancing Handbook*, 15th edition. The relevant sections are section E.3, F.4 and the guidance on accepting undertakings after *Patel* v. *Daybells* [2001] EWCA Civ 1229 in appendix IV.7.

See also the SRA warning card on undertakings updated in April 2009.

This provides that 'you must ensure that your undertakings are specific, measurable, agreed, realistic and timed.'

## 6 DISCHARGES

Lenders may use any of a variety of methods available to them for effecting a discharge. This brings uncertainty because the nature of the form of discharge used affects the timing of the availability of the discharge for registration.

The discharge may be evidenced by a DS1, an ED, an END or an e-DS1.

A buyer's solicitor may attempt to establish from the seller's solicitor the nature of the discharge that will be used in the transaction. However this is unlikely to provide certainty as to the method that will ultimately be used.

The reasons for this are:

- The seller's solicitor may not know the form of discharge that the seller's lender is proposing to use until quite a late stage in the transaction.
- The nature of discharge may change during the course of a transaction. For example, some electronic methods of discharge revert to paper if they cannot be processed electronically for some reason.

In addition, some lenders:

- operate different methods of discharge for different members within the same group
- use multiple methods of discharge that change according to the nature of the mortgage product.

Nonetheless as set out in paragraph 4 above it may assist you to request from the seller's solicitor information about the likely method of discharge to be used. It is factor that may help you to assess the risks.

From 27 July 2009, LR will make available an updated version of their Methods of Discharge Practice Guide – 31 *Discharge of charges*.

## 7  IDENTIFICATION REQUIREMENTS (ID)

When making the second application to register the paper discharge of the seller's discharge you will not need to provide a new ID form if LR has retained form ID1 or ID2 in respect of the lender for a charge being discharged by a paper DS1. This is so long as the evidence of identity is no more than three months old at the time the further application is made after early completion.

You should add a note to panel 13 of form AP1 to refer LR to the ID form you have already provided.

This is only relevant where the solicitor is not representing the discharging lender. This should already have been established in replies to TA13 Completion arrangements and requisitions, if not earlier.

You may make provision in the contract for when evidence of identity becomes more than three months old, because it will be difficult to establish, in advance, cases in which evidence is likely to be or may be more than three months old. You can provide that such provisions do not merge on completion. See Standard Conditions of Sale (4th edition) condition 7.4.

This also applies to evidence of identity for the borrower or lender for a new charge in respect of which the LR has cancelled an application.

## 8  APPLICATION OF EARLY COMPLETION

### 8.1  Transfers of Part

LR will not complete applications to register transfers of part on the basis of early completion but say they will keep the position under review. LR will requisition for a discharge of part if one is required and not lodged with an application to register a transfer of part. However LR will continue to operate the process as now without implementing early completion.

### 8.2  Charges of Part

Early completion does not apply to applications that only comprise an application for a discharge of part of a charge to be registered.

### 8.3  Remortgages

Early completion presents fewer concerns when applied to remortgages where the borrower in relation to the incoming and outgoing charges will be the same, as there will be no undertaking between sellers and buyers solicitors. However the status of the application needs to be monitored to ensure that the new lender obtains a first legal charge.

### 8.4 Leases

LR states that it already applies a form of early completion when dealing with applications to register a dispositionary first lease where there is a charge registered against the landlord's title. Although the charge is not usually discharged when a lease is granted, the absence of the chargee's consent to the grant of a lease by the landlord does not prevent the lease from being registered with absolute title.

In relation to the transfer or assignment of leases subject to a mortgage, rather than the grant of a lease, early completion will apply as at 3 above.

### 8.5 Discharges

Where the application to remove the registered charge is the only application made, and the evidence is not available to LR when the application is received LR will reject it as being substantially defective under rule 16(3) of the Land Registration Rules 2003, regardless of the method of discharge. This is because the new early completion procedures relate to applications to remove the entries relating to a registered charge where evidence of discharge is not supplied with, or prior to, the application. This is the only circumstance in which the LR will reject, rather than cancel an application.

See the following for further information:

- LR PG 50 Requisition and cancellation procedures
- LR PG 49 Return and rejection of applications for registration

## 9 FEES

### 9.1 LR fees

No further fee is payable if you need to make a further application to remove the charge entries that remain after early completion. This remains true if your further application also includes the registration of a new charge rejected under early completion, provided that you lodge a copy of the Registration Completion Sheet (RCS) sent following completion of your original application.

### 9.2 Your fees

When estimating your charges at the start of the retainer, you may wish to give advance notice of any additional work that you may have to carry out as a result of early completion. These may include likely additional LR fees, additional priority search fees and/or lodgement of restriction fees in addition to your professional charges as the operation of this policy is likely to involve you in spending additional time on each matter.

## 10 MORE INFORMATION

### 10.1 Professional conduct

The following sections of the Solicitors' Code of Conduct 2007 are relevant.

- Rule 1.01 Justice and the Rule of Law
- Rule 2 Client relations
- Rule 3 Conflict of interest
- Rule 3.07 Acting for lender and borrower in conveyancing transactions
- Rule 4.01 Duty of confidentiality

# LAND REGISTRY EARLY COMPLETION PRACTICE NOTE

- Rule 4.02 Duty of disclosure
- Rule 10 Relations with third parties

## 10.2 Legal and other requirements

- Land Registration Amendment Rules 2008 (as amended) (LRR)
- Land Registration Act 2002 (as amended) (LRA) various but see sections 16, 27(2)(a) and (f)
- Land Registration Rules 2003 (as amended) (LRR) various but see rule 114 and 115
- Fraud Act 2006
- Money Laundering Regulations 2007
- Proceeds of Crime Act 2002 (as amended)
- CML Handbook

## 10.3 Further products and support

### 10.3.1 Practice Advice Line

The Law Society provides support for solicitors on a wide range of areas of practice. Practice Advice can be contacted on 0870 606 2522 from 09:00 to 17:00 on weekdays.

### 10.3.2 Other practice notes and Law Society materials

- Mortgage fraud practice note
- Anti-money laundering practice note
- Property Section
- Land Registry Identity requirements
- Home Information Packs
- The Law Society's *Conveyancing Handbook* 16th Edition
- Land Registry Practice Bulletin 16 Early Completion (PDF)
- Land Registry Early Completion FAQs

### 10.3.3 Council of Mortgage Lenders

The CML is the trade association for the mortgage lending industry and represents first charge lenders. Not all lenders are members of the CML.

## 10.4 Status of this practice note

Practice notes are issued by the Law Society for the use and benefit of its members. They represent the Law Society's view of good practice in a particular area. They are not intended to be the only standard of good practice that solicitors can follow. You are not required to follow them, but doing so will make it easier to account to oversight bodies for your actions.

Practice notes are not legal advice, nor do they necessarily provide a defence to complaints of misconduct or of inadequate professional service. While care has been taken to ensure that they are accurate, up to date and useful, the Law Society will not accept any legal liability in relation to them.

For queries or comments on this practice note contact the Law Society's Practice Advice Service.

APPENDIX H(I)

## 10.5 Terminology in this practice note

'Completion' – LR in the context of 'early completion' use this to mean acceleration of when they will make the first changes to the register in connection with the applications received.

'You' – the solicitor making the application to LR – the applicant's solicitor.

'Charge' – may refer to more than one charge that is it includes first, second and third charges.

'Held over' – the process whereby LR puts incomplete applications to one side pending receipt of the information necessary to complete the application.

'Registration Completion Sheet' (RCS) – the new form that LR will use in place of the completion of registration letter that accompanies an application completed on the basis of early completion.

'Title Information Document' (TID) – issued by LR following completion of an application for registration with an official copy of the register. The TID explains why the official copies have been issued.

Must – a specific requirement in the Solicitors' Code of Conduct or legislation. You must comply, unless there are specific exemptions or defences provided for in the code of conduct or relevant legislation.

Should – good practice for most situations in the Law Society's view. If you do not follow this, you must be able to justify to oversight bodies why this is appropriate, either for your practice, or in the particular retainer.

May – a non-exhaustive list of options for meeting your obligations. Which option you choose is determined by the risk profile of the individual practice, client or retainer. You must be able to justify why this was an appropriate option to oversight bodies.

## 10.6 Acknowledgements

- Law Society Conveyancing and Land Law Committee
- Law Society E-Conveyancing Task Force
- Law Society Property Section

APPENDIX H(II)

# Property and registration fraud practice note[1]

## 1. INTRODUCTION

### 1.1 Who should read this practice note?

All solicitors who carry out work involving Land Registry applications.

### 1.2 What is the issue?

Fraud is on the increase and there is a rising incidence or awareness of fraudsters targeting the properties of both individuals and companies. These attacks often include identity and other types of fraud and the presentation of forged documents to Land Registry for registration. Land Registry wishes to bring these matters to the attention of the public and have issued public guides to this effect.

This practice note aims to assist you when acting in property transactions. It may also help you make your clients more aware of how they may protect their property interests against fraud and safeguard their rights as legitimate property owners on the register.

This advice is not exhaustive. Many aspects of mortgage fraud can also be adapted to commit registration fraud. For further information see the Law Society practice note on mortgage fraud.

## 2. FRAUD THREATS FOR PROPERTY TRANSACTIONS

### 2.1 Impersonation of conveyancers and conveyancing practices

Those proposing to carry out fraud may purport to:

- be a conveyancer in their own right, or
- work for an authorised practice.

If you do not know either the conveyancer or the conveyancing practice acting for another party in a matter you should check their details to help assess the risk of fraud.

When accepting identification (or any other) information from a person holding themselves out to be a conveyancer you should consider the following:

- Is the individual a conveyancer?

---

[1] © The Law Society. This practice note is as stated on 11 October 2010. Practice notes are updated by the Law Society from time to time. Solicitors are advised to check **www.lawsociety.org.uk** for the latest version.

APPENDIX H(II)

- Is the name of the signatory an identifiable registered individual within a conveyancing practice?
- Are they registered with an appropriate professional body?

The Law Society, the Solicitors Regulation Authority (SRA), the Council for Licensed Conveyors (CLC), The Institute for Legal Executives (ILEX) and other professional bodies hold such information [...]. More information is provided in the Conveyancing Handbook under 'Dealing with non-solicitors'.

Where a party is unrepresented and you are unable to confirm that sufficient steps have been taken to verify that party's identity, Land Registry requires you to provide certified identification information obtained by you or another conveyancer in respect of that party. This is explained in Land Registry's Practice Guide 67 – *Evidence of identity – conveyancers* with specimen forms.

Obtaining identification information at an early stage in the transaction may avoid difficulties or delays at a later stage. You may wish to keep a record of the steps you take. These may assist you if Land Registry or other bodies contact you to make enquiries but see [...] below on reporting fraud.

### 2.1.1 Impersonation of solicitors' firms

There have been instances where fraudulent applications have been made to Land Registry by fraudsters impersonating legitimate firms of solicitors by using forged headed paper, faxes and emails. Email addresses that are non distinct, for example hotmail addresses, are more difficult to trace.

If you receive communications from Land Registry, including any acknowledgement of an application, and you are unable to identify the client name, the property or the application reference you should contact Land Registry. It is possible that your firm name or its headed paper has been forged or misappropriated and used fraudulently by a third party, or even a member of your staff.

See [...] below on reporting fraud.

### 2.1.2 Misuse of websites

Web sites have been fraudulently set up purporting to be sites of solicitors and/or new sub-offices of legitimate firms in order to perpetrate fraud. Some firms periodically search the internet to establish if they are being targeted in this way. If you become aware of an unauthorised web presence for your practice you should notify the relevant agencies.

### 2.2 Seller and buyer frauds

Certain properties and owners are particularly susceptible to fraud. Most fraudulent activity falls into distinct categories:

- Intra-family/associate frauds which are perpetrated by family members, friends or partners.
- Third party frauds where tenants or those who have access to tenants and are able to divert post perpetrate the fraud.
- Third party frauds that constitute 'organised crime'.

### 2.2.1 Contact details

Client contact details may suggest an increased risk of fraud, such as:

# PROPERTY AND REGISTRATION FRAUD PRACTICE NOTE

- where the only contact details provided for any party are a telephone number, mobile number and/or an email address
- where a family member or associate is gifting the property and you are instructed by and meet only one party to the transaction, and only have contact with the other party by post, telephone or email
- where the address is not the subject of the transaction without obvious reason
- where the address changes occur mid-transaction without obvious reason.

There may be entirely valid reasons for all of these examples.

### 2.2.2 *Vulnerable registered owners*

Land Registry has identified that certain categories of owners may be more susceptible to registration frauds. These vulnerable registered owners include, for example, elderly owners who are in hospital or have moved into a care home. These types of owners often own properties without a legal charge. Attempts could be made to sell or charge their property by use of identity fraud.

Owners who live abroad are also particularly vulnerable to this type of fraud.

Some clients may be particularly at risk from fraudulent activity because, for example:

- they no longer live in the property and there was an acrimonious break up with a partner
- they let the property or it is empty
- they have already been the victim of identity fraud
- they are a personal representative responsible for a property where the owner has died and the property is to be sold.

## 2.3 Vulnerable properties

Land Registry has identified that certain types of properties may be particularly vulnerable to registration frauds, such as:

- unoccupied properties, whether residential or commercial
- tenanted properties
- high value properties without a legal charge
- high value properties with a legal charge in favour of an individual living overseas
- properties undergoing redevelopment.

## 2.4 Keeping addresses up to date

In order to minimise risk where there are vulnerable registered owners or vulnerable properties Land Registry advises registered proprietors to keep any addresses they have registered for service at Land Registry up to date. See Land Registry *Public Guide 2 – Keeping your address for service up to date*.

Clients intending to leave their property empty for a significant period of time, such as, for redevelopment purposes, should consider registering some other address(es) for service. (see paragraph 4.2.1).

## 3. MITIGATING FRAUD THREATS

### 3.1 Client identity

You should be aware that exercising reasonable care in viewing documents intended to establish identity may not conclusively prove that the person or company is the person or

APPENDIX H(II)

company they are purporting to be. In addition it may not be possible for you to conclusively establish that such person or company is either the registered proprietor of the relevant property or entitled to become so registered.

Even where you have followed usual professional practice the court may hold that the steps taken exposed someone to a foreseeable and avoidable risk and amounted to a breach of duty of care. See *Edward Wong Finance Co Ltd* v. *Johnson Stokes & Master* [1984] 1 AC 296.

*3.1.1 Conveyancing anti-money laundering*

Conveyancing transactions are regulated activity under the Money Laundering Regulations 2007. You must therefore take steps to:

- identify and verify your client by independent means
- identify and, on a risk-sensitive approach, verify any beneficial owners, and
- obtain information on the purpose and intended nature of the business relationship.

This last requirement means more than just finding out that they want to sell a property. It also encompasses looking at all of the information in the retainer and assessing whether it is consistent with a lawful transaction. This may include considering whether the client is actually the owner of the property they want to sell.

You should also comply with Money Laundering Regulations and Law Society general practice information.

For further information about fraud prevention see the Law Society's anti-money laundering practice note.

You may keep a record of any steps you take.

*3.1.2 Address for service at Land Registry*

Since July 2008 Land Registry has inserted an entry in the register indicating whether the registered proprietor has changed their address for service (see paragraphs 4.2 and 4.2.1 below), to alert people to the change. For example, the entry may state: 'The proprietor's address for service has been changed'. People proposing to commit fraud have been known to change the address for service registered at Land Registry as a precursor to fraud. If you see this on your client's register and are not aware of the reason for it you may ask your client why it was done.

**3.2 Surrounding circumstances**

Further factors you may consider include the following:

- Where the registered proprietor is a company, does a search at Companies House indicate that the company was incorporated after the registered proprietor was registered as the owner?
- Have you met your client face to face?
- Have you seen the original identity documents or only copies?
- Is the registered proprietor's date of birth inconsistent with their being the owner?

For example:

Someone purports to be a registered proprietor and offers identification information, but there is an inconsistency between their date of birth and information on the register.

The date appearing immediately before a proprietor's name in the proprietorship register is the date of registration of that owner:

(13.10.1970) JOHN SMITH and JANE SMITH

In this example the proprietors have been registered since 1970 and must have been at least 18 at that time. Consequently, if, in cases where you are seeing the client face to face, the person presenting the identification information appears too young, this may be a case of impersonation.

### 3.3 Company impersonation

If the company was incorporated after the registered proprietor was registered as the owner the registered proprietor is unlikely to be the legitimate owner. Despite appearing to have the same company name, the discrepancy of dates will indicate dealing with a company of the same name but not necessarily the 'real' registered proprietor. You should note that an Industrial and Provident Society that has converted to a company registered under the Companies Acts would be an exception to this situation.

One notable registration fraud involved the impersonation of an overseas company by the setting up of a UK company with the same name. If a search at Companies House states that the date of incorporation of the UK company is after the date of registration of the property in that company's name, further enquiry should be made.

The date of registration [as proprietor] is the date appearing in brackets immediately before the company name in the proprietorship register. A discrepancy without any legitimate reason may be a risk factor.

*3.3.1 Foreign companies*

Since January 1999 Land Registry has been entering the company's/corporation's country of incorporation in the proprietorship entry. In some cases this will also include the state or province of incorporation, for example incorporated in Delaware, USA. This information appears in the register immediately after the corporation's name.

If an overseas company has a registration number issued by Companies House because it has a branch or place of business in the UK, that registration number is also included in the proprietorship entry as follows:

> Proprietor:- NORDDEUTSCHE LANDESBANK GIROZENTRALE (incorporated in Germany ) (UK Regn. No. FC012190) of .............

If there is no Companies House registration number this may help you identify a registered proprietor as an overseas company, provided it was registered after January 1999. If the registered proprietor is a foreign company, a UK company with the same name is unlikely to be able to give instructions as the registered proprietor of the property.

Verification of the identity of an overseas company may require confirmation from a qualified lawyer authorised in the country of incorporation. See Land Registry Practice Guide 67 – *Evidence of identity: conveyancers*.

*3.3.2 Searching Companies House*

Where no place of incorporation and no UK company number are noted on the register, you may be able to establish the date of incorporation by making a search of Companies House. The results of searches of Companies House may assist in assessing the risk of an overseas company impersonation.

APPENDIX H(II)

### 3.4 Identity document provisions

You should be aware of the provisions relating to identity documents in the following documents:

- AML requirements
- CML Lenders' Handbook
- BSA instructions

### 3.5 Enhanced due diligence

Where you do not see a client face-to-face, the Money Laundering Regulations 2007 provide that you must undertake enhanced due diligence. Not undertaking face-to-face checks may increase the risk of the transaction being exposed to investigation by the law enforcement agencies and/or the SRA.

For further information see paragraph 4.9.1 of the Law Society's anti-money laundering practice note.

Non face-to-face transactions increase the risk of fraud and these risks may be mitigated in the following ways.

- If you are accepting instructions from one client on behalf of others or by a third party, rule 2.01(c) of the Code of Conduct requires you to check that all clients agree with the instructions given. For example, an unwary conveyancer might deal solely with the son or daughter of a registered proprietor and have no contact with the person who is the owner.
- Where you know or have reasonable grounds for believing that your instructions are affected by duress or undue influence, you should bear in mind also the provisions of rule 2.01(d).
- In the case of a third party charge created to secure debts of another, you should consider contacting the purported lender independently. If there is a purported representative for the lender, then consider contacting that representative for confirmation of the transaction. In these circumstances there is a regulatory requirement for separate representation.

Risks of fraud are increased if documents are provided to clients for execution other than in the presence of you or your staff.

In order to protect or to mitigate risk for you and your firm, you may keep a contemporaneous record of the steps you take, including the reasons why you took a particular decision and the consideration you gave to risk.

## 4. LAND REGISTRY REQUIREMENTS

### 4.1 Freedom of Information (FoI) 2000

Wherever possible Land Registry tries to assist law enforcement agencies and regulatory bodies with the prevention and detection of fraudulent activity. It is bound by the provisions of the FoI 2000, which embodies a general principle of transparency in relation to the disclosure of information within government departments. This means that requests for information, which may relate to your particular application or the conduct of your account with Land Registry, may be received from third parties.

Following an FoI request, if Land Registry has reason to believe disclosure of the information would, or would be likely to, prejudice the prevention or detection of crime, or the administration of justice, then under the provisions of s.31 FoI 2000, Land Registry will consider whether the issue of such information is in the public interest. If Land Registry considers such disclosure is not in the public interest the request may be refused under s.2(2)(b) FoI 2000.

If a person is dissatisfied with a refusal of a FoI 2000 request, an application can be made to the Information Commissioner for a decision under s.50 FoI 2000.

Where Land Registry considers such a disclosure to be in the public interest it will supply the information requested to the law enforcement agency or other body or person requesting it.

**4.2 Notices and addresses for service**

Clients need to ensure their address for service is always up to date and can be directed to Land Registry for further information. The following Land Registry public guides are available.

- *Public Guide 2 – Keeping your address for service up to date*
- *Public Guide 17 – How to safeguard against property fraud*

Where appropriate, Land Registry may require further documents or evidence, or may give any necessary or desirable notice under r.17 Land Registration Rules (LRR) 2003 (as amended) as a means of verifying information about certain transactions. This enables Land Registry to stop processing an application while further enquiries are made or law enforcement agencies notified where necessary.

If the proprietor's address for service is out of date they will not receive any such notice from Land Registry and will increase their exposure to fraudulent activity.

Some clients are more at risk than others, such as:

- buyers who will not be living at the property purchased may register multiple addresses for service. These may include those who live abroad, and landlords of commercial and residential property
- recent buyers who are moving from a property they still own may need to maintain an up-to-date address for service in relation to that property.

*4.2.1 Addresses for service*

Clients may use more than one address for service in the register. There must be at least one postal address, including an overseas address, and each registered proprietor can register up to three addresses (r.198 LRR 2003) in total.

The inclusion of additional addresses for service can give added protection to a legitimate owner as:

- the address of the property the client is selling may not be an effective address for service
- the address of the property the client is buying may not be the address where the client is contactable.

Additional addresses may be:

- another property address
- an email address, or
- the address of a professional adviser (such as a DX address).

The address of a professional adviser is most suitable for use where there is an ongoing relationship, such as, an accountant providing continuing tax advice.

APPENDIX H(II)

You should not give the address of your firm as an address for service unless you are confident that you will be able to contact your client immediately should you receive notification from Land Registry. You should be aware that such notice may not be received for many years following the conclusion of a matter and if you have acted only, for example, in the purchase of a property, you are unlikely to know whether the client has moved or sold and whether you hold up-to-date contact details for them.

Land Registry notices usually require a response within 15 days. If the address for service is outside the jurisdiction, Land Registry has no discretion to extend this time. An email address may ensure Land Registry communications reach clients even when they are away from their properties, or where post is at risk of interception.

### 4.3 Indemnity

Schedule 8 of the Land Registration Act (LRA) 2002 (as amended) provides for the payment of indemnity for loss suffered by reason of (among other things) the rectification of the register and certain mistakes in the register.

Under Schedule 8, paragraph 5(1) (b), no indemnity is payable if the loss is wholly as a result of the claimant's lack of proper care. Under Schedule 8, paragraph 5(2), any indemnity will be reduced if the loss is partly as a result of the claimant's lack of proper care.

Land Registry may seek to limit its indemnity in certain circumstances where it considers that the conveyancer failed to make reasonable checks in relation to identity.

There is case law which establishes that a lack of proper care by a conveyancer will be attributable to their client, and may therefore lead to a reduction in any indemnity payable to the client. An example of a case in which delayed notification by a conveyancer to Land Registry led to such a reduction is *Prestige Properties Ltd* v. *Scottish Provident Institution and another* [2002] EWHC 330 (Ch).

## 5. REPORTING FRAUD

### 5.1 Professional requirements

Rule 4 of the Solicitors' Code of Conduct deals with confidentiality and disclosure and your obligations when considering whether disclosure to a third party is necessary or appropriate. In particular Rule 4.01 sets out the fundamental duty that the affairs of your client(s) and former client(s) must be kept confidential except where disclosure is required or permitted by law or by the client/former client.

The SRA Guidance (see notes 9 to 19) to Rule 4 describes the exceptional circumstances when disclosure of confidential information is required or permitted; for example, where statute requires disclosure to specific government or other bodies, or in order to comply with Proceeds of Crime Act (POCA) 2002 and Money Laundering Regulations 2007, or where the solicitor's conduct is under investigation by the SRA or the Solicitors Disciplinary Tribunal.

#### 5.1.1 *Disclosure*

Where disclosure may be permitted or required by law, you must ensure that you understand the scope of your obligation in the absence of the client's specific consent, ie by considering the relevant provisions of the statutory power, and whether privileged information is protected from disclosure. You should only provide such information as you are strictly required by law to disclose.

Disclosure of confidential information which is unauthorised by your client or by the law could lead to disciplinary proceedings against you and could render you liable to a civil action by your client arising out of the misuse of confidential information.

### 5.1.2 Duty of confidentiality

The duty of confidentiality is not applicable if the retainer with the client is tainted by fraud. Confidentiality does not apply to information acquired by a solicitor where they are being used by a client to facilitate the commission of a crime or fraud, because that is not within the scope of a professional retainer. You should judge the likelihood of such an occurrence in the light of your client's explanations and any other relevant factors.

### 5.1.3 Other considerations

The other conduct and legal issues which you will need to consider in relation to this section are the following.

- Rule 1 – core duties.
- Rule 2.01 – taking on and ceasing to act for clients.
- Rule 5.01 – supervision and management responsibilities.
- Rule 20 – rights and obligations of practice.
- Legal professional privilege.

In April 2009 the SRA issued property fraud and money laundering warning cards for solicitors to help you when assessing risk.

You should therefore consider notifying Land Registry if you identify a registration fraud. If you are acting for a victim of fraud or someone you believe is a victim of fraud you should consider notifying Land Registry at the earliest opportunity subject to the other obligations set out in this paragraph 5.

If, after careful consideration of your professional obligations, you have evidence that you or someone else has been a victim of a fraud or that someone is attempting to commit a fraud, you may also decide that it is in the public interest to report that fraud. [...]

### 5.2 Money laundering and disclosure to Serious Organised Crime Agency (SOCA)

If you know or suspect that a fraud has been committed and a person is in possession of criminal property, you must consider the provisions of Proceeds of Crime Act (POCA) 2002.

The person in possession of the criminal property does not have to be your client, and you do not actually have to be involved in the transaction. In those circumstances you must still consider section 332 of POCA 2002 and whether you need to make a disclosure to SOCA to avoid committing an offence.

A disclosure to SOCA is only a defence to money laundering offences; it is not a crime report. You may need to make a separate report about the fraud to law enforcement agencies. See [...] the Law Society's anti-money laundering practice note.

You should consider implications regarding the offence of 'tipping off' under POCA 2002 if you have included information about the making of a SAR in reporting the fraud to law enforcement agencies.

While the provision of this information to such bodies is not required by law, a key element of the offence of tipping off is the likelihood of prejudicing an investigation. This risk is small when disclosing to law enforcement agencies, or to an appropriate person at the Land Registry. There is also a specific defence of making a disclosure for the purposes of preventing a money laundering offence.

Read more about the money laundering offences and tipping off offences in chapter 5 of the Law Society's anti-money laundering practice note.

Read more about how to make a report to SOCA in chapter 8 of the Law Society's anti-money laundering practice note.

APPENDIX H(II)

## 6. CIVIL LIABILITY

### 6.1 Land Registry's rights of recourse

Land Registry has statutory rights to recover money it has paid out by way of indemnity. Under Schedule 8, paragraphs 10(1)(b) and (2)(a) of LRA 2002 it is entitled to enforce any right of action which a person to whom it has paid indemnity would have had if that person had not been indemnified.

Similarly, under Schedule 8, paragraphs 10(1)(b) and (2)(b), it is entitled to enforce any rights of action which a person in whose favour the register has been rectified would have been entitled to enforce if the register had not been rectified. The registrar may have a right of recourse against a conveyancer under either head. However, Land Registry's policy is that it does not seek recovery from a conveyancer who has not been at fault, even though there may be circumstances where, strictly, it would have a right to do so.

### 6.2 Contractual liability

You should consider whether you have complied with the terms of your retainer and other professional obligations. For example, have you given any undertakings to obtain the signature of a particular person? You should also consider if you have given any warranty to a party to the transaction (other than your client) that you have the authority to act for a person in the transaction. Case law illustrates the circumstances in which the liability for breach of warranty can create an absolute liability or one actionable only on proof of negligence. See the following cases.

- *Penn v. Bristol & West Building Society and others* [1997] 3 All ER 47.
- *Zwebner v. The Mortgage Corporation* [1998] PNLR 769.
- *Midland Bank v. Cox McQueen* [1999] 1 Lloyds Rep PN 223.
- *Halifax Plc v. Espley and others*. QBD ( Leeds ). 23 May 2000 (Unreported).

## 7. MORE INFORMATION

### 7.1 Professional conduct

The following sections of the Solicitors' Code of Conduct 2007 are relevant to this issue:

- Rule 1.01 Justice and the Rule of Law
- Rule 2 Client relations
- Rule 3 Conflict of interests
- Rule 3.16 Acting for lender and borrower in conveyancing transactions
- Rule 4.01 Duty of confidentiality
- Rule 4.02 Duty of disclosure

### 7.2 Legal and other requirements

- Land Registration Rules 2008 (as amended)
- Land Registration Act 2002 (as amended)
- Land Registration Rules 2003 (as amended)
- Fraud Act 2006
- Money Laundering Regulations 2007
- Proceeds of Crime Act 2002 (as amended)
- CML Lenders' Handbook

## PROPERTY AND REGISTRATION FRAUD PRACTICE NOTE

### 7.3 Products and services

*7.3.1 Law Society publications*

- The Law Society mortgage fraud practice note
- The Law Society anti-money laundering practice note
- The Conveyancing Handbook 17th Edition
- The Conveyancing Handbook Forms and Procedures, 4th Edition
- SRA property fraud warning card
- SRA money laundering warning card

*7.3.2 Land Registry guides*

- Practice Guide 67 – *Evidence of identity: conveyancers*
- Public Guide 2 – *Keeping your address for service up-to-date*
- Public Guide 17 – *How to safeguard against property fraud*
- Public Guide 20 – *Evidence of identity: non-conveyancers*
- Public Guide 22 – *Keeping your name in the register up to date*

*7.3.3 Practice Advice line*

The Law Society provides support for solicitors on a wide range of areas of practice. Practice Advice can be contacted on 0870 606 2522 from 9am to 5pm on weekdays.

*7.3.4 Land Registry enquiries*

For queries relating to Land Registry please contact Land Registry on 0844 892 1111.

*7.3.5 Professional bodies*

- The Law Society
- Solicitors Regulation Authority
- Council for Licensed Conveyancers
- Institute of Legal Executives

### 7.4 Status of this practice note

This practice note has been prepared jointly by Land Registry and the Law Society.

Practice notes are issued by the Law Society for the use and benefit of its members. They represent the Law Society's view of good practice in a particular area. They are not intended to be the only standard of good practice that solicitors can follow. You are not required to follow them, but doing so will make it easier to account to oversight bodies for your actions.

Practice notes are not legal advice, nor do they necessarily provide a defence to complaints of misconduct or of inadequate professional service. While care has been taken to ensure that they are accurate, up to date and useful, the Law Society will not accept any legal liability in relation to them.

### 7.5 Terminology in this practice note

'**the register**' means the register of title, except in the context of cautions against first registration ( s.132 LRA 2002)

'**conveyancer**' means a solicitor, a licensed conveyancer within the meaning of s.11(2), Administration of Justice Act 1985, a Fellow of the Institute of Legal Executives (r217(c),

LRR 2003), a barrister (r217(d), LRR 2003), a duly certificated notary public (r217(e), LRR 2003), or a registered European lawyer (r217(e), LRR 2003)

'**legitimate owner**' means the rightful claimant to the land or the interest in land whose rights require protection, which could include someone with the right to apply for first registration; a registered proprietor; a registered proprietor of a charge; or someone with the benefit of an interest such as a notice or restriction. See LRA 2002 for definitions

'**property**' means any land or interest capable of registration under LRA 2002

'**criminal property**' means property that:

    (a)    constitutes a person's benefit from criminal conduct or it represents such a benefit (in whole or part and whether directly or indirectly), and

    (b)    the alleged offender knows or suspects that it constitutes or represents such a benefit (Section 340(3) of the Proceeds of Crime Act 2002)

'**organised crime**' means two or more people involved in continuing significant illegal activities; such a group is capable of defending its members with violence, coercion or corruption; and more than £1m in criminal proceeds has been generated

'**law enforcement agencies**' means:

    (a)    the Commissioners or any other government department
    (b)    the Scottish Administration
    (c)    any other person who is charged with the duty of investigating offences or charging offenders, or
    (d)    any other person who is engaged outside the United Kingdom in the carrying on of activities similar to any carried on by SOCA or a police force

*(Section 3(4)(a) of the Serious Organised Crime and Police Act 2005)*

'**must**' – a specific requirement in the Solicitors' Code of Conduct or legislation. You must comply, unless there are specific exemptions or defences provided for in the code of conduct or relevant legislation

'**should**' – good practice for most situations in the Law Society's view. If you do not follow this, you must be able to justify to oversight bodies why this is appropriate, either for your practice, or in the particular retainer

'**may**' – a non-exhaustive list of options for meeting your obligations. Which option you choose is determined by the risk profile of the individual practice, client or retainer. You must be able to justify why this was an appropriate option to oversight bodies

## 7.6 Acknowledgements

The Law Society and Land Registry have worked in close collaboration on the production of this practice note.

# APPENDIX I

# Accepting undertakings on completion following the Court of Appeal decision in *Patel* v. *Daybells*[1]

### Accepting undertakings on completion

The first instance decision in *Patel* v. *Daybells* [2000] All ER(D) 1004 caused consternation among conveyancers. It held that it was negligent for a buyer's solicitor to accept an undertaking for Form 53 (now DS1), save in exceptional circumstances. The Court of Appeal ([2001] EWCA Civ 1229) has now upheld the decision that the solicitor in the case was not negligent, but reversed the reasoning – the acceptance of a solicitor's undertaking for a DS1 will not normally be negligent. But does this mean a return to business as usual?

The Court of Appeal held that 'conformity to a common (or even universal) professional practice is not an automatic defence against liability; the practice must be demonstrably reasonable and responsible'. This involves considering the risks involved and how to avoid them. The Court of Appeal was satisfied that the legal profession had considered the risks of accepting an undertaking and that in the standard case it was reasonable to rely on the existence of compulsory insurance, the Compensation Fund and the summary procedure for enforcing undertakings when assessing the extent of that risk. Other relevant factors were: the Council of Mortgage Lenders' advice to its members to discharge a mortgage even where insufficient funds were sent, if this was due to the lender's error; and the problems which would ensue if the buyer's solicitor had to communicate directly with the seller's lender.

### Exceptional cases

The 'exceptional circumstances' in which it might be negligent for a buyer's solicitor to accept an undertaking were not specified by the Court of Appeal, although the court made it clear that the fact that the seller's solicitor was a sole practitioner did not make the transaction exceptional.

The court referred in detail to the expert evidence on behalf of the buyer's solicitor that it would not be normal or advisable to rely on an undertaking in two situations, but did not expressly endorse these as the relevant 'exceptional circumstances'. The two situations mentioned are:

---

[1]  © The Law Society. Prepared by the Law Society's Conveyancing and Land Law Committee in May 2002.

- Where the amount required to redeem the seller's mortgage exceeds the minimum level of solicitors' indemnity insurance (currently [£2m] per claim); or
- Where the mortgagee is not a member of the Council of Mortgage Lenders.

**Minimising the risks in exceptional cases**

The risk of accepting an undertaking for a DS1 is that it might not be forthcoming (e.g. because of the fraud or negligence of the seller's solicitor or because of problems in identifying the amount required to redeem the mortgage). Default by the seller's solicitor is dealt with by the requirement for compulsory insurance and, ultimately, the Compensation Fund. Only where the figures exceed the compulsory level of insurance might the buyer's solicitor need to take additional steps to deal with that risk. The risk of a dispute with the lender should not normally be a problem where the lender is a member of the CML. Even disputes not covered by the CML's advice may not put the buyer's solicitor at risk: the Law Society's recommended form of undertaking puts an absolute obligation on the seller's solicitor to discharge the relevant mortgage. It is therefore the seller's solicitor who is at risk if the DS1 is not forthcoming: his obligations can be summarily enforced and are backed by compulsory insurance and in certain cases, the Compensation Fund.

In each of the exceptional cases mentioned in *Patel* v. *Daybells* the matter comes back to the safeguards put in place by the profession. The only variable is the level of insurance cover and that is only relevant in the case of large mortgages. Normally the buyer's solicitor does not know the amount of the debt (and the Court of Appeal disapproved of the idea that the buyer's solicitor should have to make such enquiries). It is common to ask in preliminary enquiries for confirmation that the sale price exceeds the amount secured on the mortgage. Provided the sale price is not more than [£2m], such confirmation should give the buyer's solicitor the necessary comfort to accept an undertaking from the seller's solicitor. In larger transactions the buyer's solicitor may wish to take additional steps before or instead of accepting an undertaking.

- The buyer's solicitor could ask the seller's solicitor to get express written confirmation from the lender that he has been appointed the lender's agent for the receipt of the redemption money. This places the risk of default or dispute with the lender and avoids the buyer having to investigate either the details of the mortgage or the seller's solicitor's insurance.
- The buyer's solicitor could insist on sending the redemption money direct to the lender. The buyer's solicitor should ask to see the redemption statement as independent evidence of the figure. The Court of Appeal disapproved of the buyer making such enquiries in the standard case but in an exceptional case, where large sums are involved, this may be inevitable. As this information is confidential to the seller, the seller's solicitor should get instructions before revealing it. However, this solution does not deal with the problem of a dispute over the amount required to redeem. It may also be difficult to arrange in the case of an 'all moneys' mortgage. If this course is followed, Standard Condition 6.7 should be amended (or, if using the Standard Commercial Property Conditions, expand condition 6.7). In either case, the issue must be addressed before exchange (or if using the Standard Commercial Property Conditions, expand condition 8.7).
- Where the amount of the mortgage debt exceeds the minimum indemnity insurance (as will often be the case in commercial transactions), a buyer's solicitor might only accept an undertaking for DS1 if coupled with a warranty from the seller's solicitor that his insurance cover exceeds the amount required to redeem the mortgage.

- Finally, there is no obligation to accept an undertaking in place of performance of the obligation. Indeed, solicitors have often been unwilling to accept an undertaking for the DS1 in the case of a mortgage to a non-institutional or overseas lender or in the case of a private loan. However, if that is the buyer's solicitor's position, a contract condition that the DS1 must be available on completion will be necessary. In many cases this will not be a realistic option as institutional lenders' procedures do not include issuing the DS1 in escrow.

Before the buyer's solicitor accepts an undertaking where the expert evidence in *Patel* v. *Daybells* stated it would not be normal practice to do so, it is essential to explain the risks to the buyer and get clear instructions that the buyer is willing to take them.

Even where the lender is separately represented, the buyer's solicitor should consider whether there are any exceptional circumstances making it unwise (or potentially negligent) to accept an undertaking (or at least without evidence of the lender's solicitor's authority to accept the redemption money).

## ENDs

The use of Electronic Notifications of Discharge (END) presents a particular problem as there is never a paper DS1 to be handed over: the buyer's solicitor is always reliant on an undertaking by the seller's solicitor to forward the redemption money and the END form to the lender, who then sends the discharge notification directly to the Land Registry. Even where the transaction might fall into the category of exceptional cases the buyer's solicitor will ultimately have no choice but to accept the undertaking and will have to take such steps as are available (e.g. split payments, evidence of the seller's solicitor's authority, evidence of sufficient insurance cover).